MURDEROUS

The Phantom X

SSSH!

KJARTAN POSKITT

Illustrated by
Philip Reeve

Hippo

To Marina Chester with special thanks for all her help
and encouragement on the Murderous Maths series.

Scholastic Children's Books,
Commonwealth House, 1–19 New Oxford Street,
London WC1A 1NU, UK

A division of Scholastic Ltd
London ~ New York ~ Toronto ~ Sydney ~ Auckland
Mexico City ~ New Delhi ~ Hong Kong

Published in the UK by Scholastic Ltd, 2003

Text copyright © Kjartan Poskitt 2003
Illustrations copyright © Philip Reeve 2003

ISBN 0 439 97729 0

Typeset by MRules
Printed and bound by Nørhaven Paperback A/S, Denmark

4 6 8 10 9 7 5

The right of Kjartan Poskitt and Philip Reeve to be identified
as the author and illustrator of this work respectively has been
asserted by them in accordance with the Copyright, Designs and
Patents Act, 1988.

CONTENTS

.MURDEROUS MATHS.

Join the Murderous Maths gang for more fun, games and tips at **www.murderousmaths.co.uk**

THE SECRET WEAPON

You haven't seen me before and, after this book, I hope for your sake we never meet again, because I'm dangerous to be seen with. In fact, just to be safe, before you read on check there's no one looking over your shoulder.

All clear? Right then, here's the situation. Maths is one long fierce battle in which we're all being attacked by an army of different problems. Luckily, most of them are little sums that you can solve in your head. Then, for really tough sums, you can bang the numbers into a calculator and read off the answer. But sometimes you have to do sums and you aren't told what the numbers are! How can you put a number into a calculator when you don't know what it is? What do you do when you're facing the UNKNOWN?

It's usually a job for ... the Phantom X.

PLEASE SING DRAMATICALLY TO YOURSELF AT THIS POINT. DAH DAH DAHHH!

I hide in the shadows, always ready to leap out and solve the unsolvable, calculate the incalculable, and unravel the un-unravelled. But as the universe expands and the problems multiply, I could use some help from you.

Are you sure that nobody has followed you down the page? Yes? Good. Then it's time to introduce my secret weapon – algebra.

ONCE AGAIN PLEASE! DAH DAH DAHHH!

A lot of people get so scared by unknowns that they run away screaming, but I'm hoping that you've got what it takes to join me in challenging unknowns and beating them. As you read this book, I'll be following you. Then, when we reach the end, we'll see if you're ready to defeat one of the nastiest bits of algebra ever – algebra that

NORMAL NUMBERS:
$5^2 + 23 \times 4$
THE UNKNOWNS:
$2a^2 + 5ab - 3b^2$

ARGH!

threatens to smash the whole fabric of maths apart and destroy the universe as we know it.

That's all I have to say for now apart from ... thanks. It's good to know that in future I won't be facing the unknowns alone.

WHAT IS ALGEBRA?

Algebra is a way of doing sums when you don't know what all the numbers are – so you use letters instead. Here's an example:

$$(q_1 - q_0)^{\frac{1}{6}} = p\left(\frac{3\sqrt{y+2z}}{7\Omega - 9\cdot47} - 8(y^2 - \Omega)^{\frac{2}{5}}\right) + 1$$

Don't panic! That's a bit of super-tough algebra which the Evil Gollarks use to guide their mighty Space Assailer across the galaxy.

You'll probably never need to use that bit of algebra, which is just as well.

Needless to say, Gollark algebra is far cleverer than Gollarks are so we'll leave them to it.

As we've got a lot more sense, we'll stick to stuff we can understand. How about this:

$$c = 16$$

That looks a lot easier but there's just one small question – what is it trying to tell us? The whole point of algebra is that you have to know what the letters mean. In this case "c" represents the number of legs on a normal caterpillar.

Aha! That's fine as long as you know that caterpillars have 16 legs. But suppose you didn't know?

(And be honest – you didn't know until you just read it here, did you?)

OF COURSE I KNOW HOW MANY LEGS I'VE GOT!

Yes, but if you weren't a caterpillar you wouldn't know so you could just write down "*c*". If you don't know what number "*c*" is supposed to represent then it's called an **unknown**.

Hot Tips! As we see how algebra works, the most useful bits are marked with a ⊗.

AND WHAT ARE THE MOST USELESS BITS MARKED WITH?

The most useless bits will be marked with a SQUISHED CATERPILLAR.

⊗ **All letters and numbers are either positive or negative. Negative numbers are less than zero and always have a "–" in front. The negative sign is part of the number.**

If you had a sum like $12 = 7 + 9 - 4$, then -4 is negative. If you move the sum around to get $12 = 7 - 4 + 9$, you'll see that the "–" has to stay with the 4 otherwise the sum doesn't work. The minus sign was glued on in that great maths factory in the sky and there's not a thing you can do about it.

If a number isn't negative then it must be positive.

Obviously the + 9 is positive, but so are the 12 and the 7. To make things really clear, people should write + 12 = + 7 + 9 − 4, but they don't usually bother writing "+" by the first numbers in a sum. However, even if you can't see the "+" sign in front of a number, it's still there because it was also glued on in that great maths factory in the sky. And there's not a thing you can do about that either.

ⓧ When you multiply two numbers together, make sure the answer has the correct sign! If the signs are the same, the answer is positive. If the signs are different the answer is negative.

+3 × +2 = +6 signs are the same
+3 × −2 = −6 signs are different
−3 × +2 = −6 signs are different
−3 × −2 = +6 signs are the same
(so two "−" signs become "+")

Letters, numbers and the mutant caterpillar
You can use letters in almost exactly the same way as numbers. If you have five caterpillars, how many legs will there be? The answer is 5 × 16 but if you didn't know how many legs each caterpillar had, you could put 5c.

HA HA! YOU MISSED A X SIGN IN THERE!

No, we haven't. You *could* write $5 \times c$ but as there's lots of multiplying in algebra, people hardly ever bother putting the multiplication signs next to letters. This is partly because "$\times$" looks a bit like the letter "*x*" but mainly because it's simply not cool and people would laugh at you.

By the way, when you have $5c$, the "5" bit is called the **coefficient**.

❌ **It's important to check if a coefficient is positive (+) or negative (–). As this 5 hasn't got a "–" sign, you can assume it's positive. If this sum were more complicated, it would help to say that the coefficient of $5c$ is "+5".**

PAH! THAT'S NOT USEFUL, THAT'S COMPLETELY USELESS!

Oh, really? Then if it's useless, we'd better mark it with a squished caterpillar...

ALL RIGHT! IT'S SO FANTASTICALLY USEFUL I DON'T KNOW HOW I'VE LIVED WITHOUT IT! HAPPY NOW?

Good grief! Murderous Maths fans are patient people, but there's only so much cheek we can take from a caterpillar. Maybe it's time to do a little experiment. Let's grab a caterpillar and slice it into 4 equal bits.

OI! COME BACK!

How many legs will each bit have? In numbers, it's $16 \div 4$ which you can also write as $\frac{16}{4}$. With algebra you hardly ever use dividing signs either, so you would put $\frac{c}{4}$. By the way, what do you think the coefficient of $\frac{c}{4}$ is? The answer is $\frac{1}{4}$ because $\frac{c}{4}$ is the same as $\frac{1}{4} \times c$.

Suppose you have six of these caterpillar bits, each with $\frac{c}{4}$ legs and you graft them all together to make a mutant minibeast – how many legs will the mutant have? It's $6 \times \frac{c}{4}$. Just like normal fractions, you only multiply the top number by the multiplying number, so the answer will be $\frac{6c}{4}$. And again, just like normal fractions, you can cancel out. This means, if you can see a number that divides into both top and bottom, you should divide it. In this case the number 2 will divide into both top and bottom so you get $\frac{3c}{2}$.

Just to prove our sums work, here's our mutant caterpillar...

Each section has four legs, so you can work out how many legs there are. It's 6 × 4 = 24. We can also check our little formula $\frac{3c}{2}$ by swapping the "c", that stands for the number of legs a caterpillar has, for 16. We get $\frac{3 \times 16}{2} = \frac{48}{2} = 24$ which is what we hoped for.

When the unknown enters the equation
Let's go back to the sad old days when you had no idea how many legs a normal caterpillar had...

There you are one evening, unable to read a book or watch the telly because your mind is racked with agonizing ignorance regarding caterpillar legs. Suddenly, you hear a loud *snap* from under your kitchen sink. You investigate and see that a caterpillar has just crawled over an old mousetrap and got itself chopped into two bits. One bit has seven legs and the other bit has nine legs. You can make a little equation to work out what "c" is.

$$c = 7 + 9$$

This equation only has one unknown, which is c (the number of legs a caterpillar has).

Dear Murderous Maths,
I've already worked out what
c is. Do I win a prize?
Yours greedily,
Miss E. Pance

No. Honestly! By now *everybody* reading this book knows what c is. We're just pretending we don't know to show how equations work. We're starting with a simple one but equations will be getting *tough* very shortly. Just have a look at page 44. See? By the time we get there, you'll understand it all, so don't worry.

In the meantime, here's the bit that's important:

❌ If we've got one equation with one unknown, we can solve it.

Don't hurt your head on this one, but if you start with $c = 7 + 9$ and take it steadily you'll find that $c = 16$.

Suddenly you get a great idea for an invention! You're going to make a toothbrush that uses the legs off woodlice for bristles.

The only problem is that you don't know the number of legs a woodlouse has, so when you write out all your secret plans you just call this number "w". But then you discover a secret formula:

$$w = c - 2$$

This time, you've got an equation with *two* unknowns, so sadly you can't do much about it ... until you glance back up the page and realize that we said "c" represents the number of legs on a caterpillar. This is exciting!

As we already know $c = 16$ we can substitute 16 for "c" in the equation. We get $w = 16 - 2$ and so we can see that $w = 14$. (And yes, that IS the number of legs on a woodlouse. We had a pretty itchy time in the Murderous Maths office counting them.)

❌A tiny short cut: as the left-hand side of the equation stayed the same (it was just w) we don't need to write out $w = 16 - 2$ and then $w = 14$ separately. We can save time by just putting $w = 16 - 2 = 14$.

When you multiply letters, you just put them next to each other. Suppose you have a giant monster woodlouse and it grabs a caterpillar with each of its legs. How many caterpillar legs does it have in total?

The woodlouse has w legs. Each leg grabs a caterpillar with c legs. So, the total number of caterpillar legs it has grabbed is $w \times c = wc$.

Suppose there are four *mega* monster woodlice and with each mega leg they can grab three caterpillars? The total number of caterpillar legs grabbed will be $4w \times 3c$, which comes to $12wc$. Notice you can multiply the numbers, and just shove the letters together at the end.

Now, suppose that there are four mega monster woodlice, each grabbing three caterpillars with each leg AND a lawn mower comes along and mashes the whole lot into a paste before dolloping it out into 48 absolutely equal little lumps.

How many caterpillar legs will be in each lump? It's $\frac{12wc}{48}$ but you can divide the top and the bottom by 12 to become $\frac{wc}{4}$.

As we know what "w" and "c" are, we can even work it out. It's $\frac{16 \times 14}{4} = 16 \times 14 \div 4 = 56$ legs. But don't take our word for it. Go out and get some monster woodlice, a load of caterpillars, and a lawnmower...

(After you've done a few Murderous Maths experiments, even the most *horrible* science is going to be a bit dull.)

Just in case you didn't realize, "c" only represented the legs on a caterpillar in this chapter. When you come across "c" at another time it may represent something completely different such as the cost of cheese or the speed of light. And next time you see "w", it could be the number of wings on a mutant butterfly. So keep your brain on full alert…

THE SLAUGHT-O-MART EQUATIONS

Let's join Grizelda the Grisly on a typical shopping trip at the Slaught-o-Mart. Grizelda wants to buy a rather nice bow with a matching quiver for the arrows. She doesn't know how much each item costs, but she'd still like to know how to work out the total. We could explain it like this:

> Grizelda's total will be the price of the bow plus the price of the quiver.

But that's a bit long-winded so instead of Grizelda's total we'll just put "G". Instead of "price of bow" we'll put "b" and instead of "price of quiver" we'll put "q". Now we can make it into a crisp little equation:

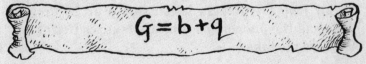

$$G = b + q$$

As Grizelda doesn't know what the prices are and she doesn't know what her total is, her little equation has *three* unknowns. This means it can't be solved.

Calm down! Although we can't do much with the equation right now, it does explain exactly how to work out the total cost as soon as we know what b and q are. Let's look in the window.

Aha! This tells us that we can swap "b" for 14 and we can swap "q" for 5 in our equation. We get:

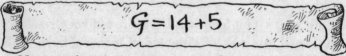

$$G = 14 + 5$$

Now we've just got one unknown, so rather excitingly we can work out the answer: $G = 19$.

But just as Grizelda is handing over 19 groats, Mungoid the Jungoid pops in. He realizes Grizelda's careless mistake.

Mungoid buys a quiver and all of the arrows left in the shop. It turns out there are 15 of them, so what will Mungoid's total cost be? We'll call his total "*M*" and the cost of each arrow "*a*". Here's the equation:

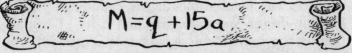

$$M = q + 15a$$

"*q*" is still the cost of a quiver, which is 5 groats, but we won't know what Mungoid spends until we know what "*a*" is...

Now we can swap "*q*" for 5 and "*a*" for 2 to get:

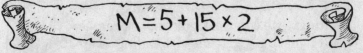

$$M = 5 + 15 \times 2$$

You'll see there are two sums here – one is adding and one is multiplying.

⊗ Always multiply or divide before you add or subtract.

So we get $M = 5 + 30 = 35$

(If the shopkeeper had added the $5 + 15$ before he had multiplied the 15×2 he'd have got $M = 20 \times 2 = 40$. Mungoid would have found himself paying 5 groats more than he should have done, and overcharging barbarians is not a good idea.)

Bring on the brackets

Meanwhile, at the back of the shop, Captain Cancel needs to buy some camouflaged underwear for his Valiant Vector Warriors. (He had a lot of trouble finding the camouflage department because it was camouflaged. It was disguised as an ice cream van.)

Each warrior needs one vest, two pairs of pants and four socks. (You buy socks one at a time in this shop. That's just in case you have an odd number of legs.) If the costs of each item are "v", "p" and "s" and the total cost of each man's outfit is "E" then we can say: $E = v + 2p + 4s$.

The captain has 13 men, so how much will 13 outfits cost? That's simple enough. It's 13E, which is the same as 13 lots of $v + 2p + 4s$. We can show this by using brackets:

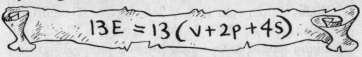

$$13E = 13(v + 2p + 4s)$$

Putting things in brackets means that they all have to be treated together as one solid lump. You can't just move one bit outside the brackets and leave the rest. The number leaning against the front of the bracket is the coefficient and here it's 13.

Getting rid of brackets

❌ **To get rid of the brackets everything inside the bracket has to be multiplied by the coefficient. (This is often called multiplying out.)**

PSST! WATCH OUT FOR INVISIBLE COEFFICIENTS!

If you have $(p + 4m)$, the coefficient of the bracket is +1. We could write it like this: +1$(p + 4m)$. However, as multiplying by +1 doesn't affect anything, we don't usually bother writing it in. But how about the coefficient of $-(3g + 2j)$? Here the coefficient is -1, so when you multiply the bracket out you get $-1 \times 3g + -1 \times 2j$ which makes $-3g - 2j$.

23

With $13(v + 2p + 4s)$, to get rid of the brackets you need to multiply +13 by the v and then the $2p$ and then the $4s$.

No, because you'd get $13E = 13v + 2p + 4s$. That's as good as saying that your 13 men only need 13 vests, two pairs of pants and four socks for ALL of them. It could be a bit chilly.

Like we said, you have to multiply *everything* in the brackets by the number outside. You'll find that $13E = 13(v + 2p + 4s) = 13v + 26p + 52s$. So the captain will need 13 vests, 26 pairs of pants and 52 socks.

Now let's look at the prices:

VEST = 5 GROATS

SOCK = 2 GROATS

PANTS = 3 GROATS

This tells us that $v = 5$, $p = 3$ and $s = 2$.

When you swap the letters for the prices, you get $13E = 13 \times 5 + 26 \times 3 + 52 \times 2$. Remember that you've always got to multiply and divide before adding and subtracting, so we get $13E = 65 + 78 + 104 = 247$. So the total cost for 13 soldiers' underwear is 247 groats.

By the way, if you know what numbers the letters are equal to, there's another way to get rid of the brackets. Now we know what "v", "p" and "s" are, we can climb inside the bracket and turn $(v + 2p + 4s)$ into $(5 + 2 \times 3 + 4 \times 2)$ and then go and get the final answer. This is how the whole equation changes bit by bit...

Swap the letters for the numbers inside the brackets and get: $13E = 13(5 + 2 \times 3 + 4 \times 2)$

Do the multiplying inside the brackets to get: $13E = 13(5 + 6 + 8)$

Do the adding in the brackets to get: $13E = 13(19)$

Remember the last tip we had: to get rid of brackets, you multiply the number outside by everything inside. As we've only got 19 inside, we can now get rid of the brackets and finish with: $13E = 13 \times 19 = 247$.

It doesn't matter which way you do it, the bill for the camouflaged underwear will still be 247 groats.

After the captain paid for the underwear, he had 160 groats left, and so he decided that each warrior could use a new tin hat too. Let's call the price marked on each hat "h" so 13 hats would cost $13h$. The question is, how much change will the Captain have out of his 160 groats? If we call his change C we can say that $C = 160 - 13h$.

But there's good news for the Captain...

HATS ARE ON SPECIAL OFFER – THEY ARE 3 GROATS LESS THAN THE MARKED PRICE.

As each hat is reduced by 3 groats, the cost of each hat is $(h - 3)$. So, the cost of 13 hats is $13(h - 3)$, and $C = 160 - 13(h - 3)$.

Before we check the price marked on the hats, let's see what happens if we get rid of the brackets. First of all, let's check the coefficient of the bracket. It's -13 which is *minus* 13.

❌ **Remember that a minus sign is part of the coefficient! (It was glued on in that great maths factory in the sky etc...)**

So, when we get rid of the brackets, we need to multiply the -13 by both things in the bracket.

The first bit is easy enough, it's $-13 \times h = -13h$. For the second bit, we are multiplying two negative numbers which means we get a positive answer. $-13 \times -3 = +39$. When we put the whole thing together we get: $C = 160 - 13(h - 3) = 160 - 13h + 39$.

We can move the numbers around as long as we keep their signs with them: $C = 160 + 39 - 13h = 199 - 13h$.

All we need to do now is check what price is marked on the hats.

Therefore, $h = 15$. Let's see what change the Captain should get: $C = 199 - 13h = 199 - 13 \times 15 = 199 - 195 = 4$

You might think it's strange that the negative number in the brackets became positive when the brackets disappeared, so let's check the answer another way. We know the hats are marked at 15 groats, but they are reduced by 3 groats each. Therefore the Captain is paying $15 - 3 = 12$ groats per hat. He buys 13 hats, so in total he spends $13 \times 12 = 156$ groats. So out of his 160 groats, he will have $160 - 156 = 4$ groats change. It works!

There's just one thing left puzzling the captain...

Thag investigates

Meanwhile, Urgum the Axeman has caused a bit of a panic because he's been browsing in the cannon section. The news of this barbaric shopping bonanza has reached Princess Laplace who has sent Thag the Mathemagician to investigate exactly who's buying what. Thag is lurking behind the spear display and quickly jots down a little equation.

Thag's equation shows how to work out U, which is Urgum's total cost. Here's what the other letters stand for: c is the cost of a cannon, x is the number of cannons he bought, g is the cost of a Goresplatt cannonball and y is the number of cannonballs.

Luckily for Thag, there's enough information for him to replace most of these letters with numbers: $U = 104$, $c = 28$, $x = 2$, $g = 3$. The equation turns into $104 = 2 \times 28 + y \times 3$. Remember, you always multiply before you add, which means you finish with: $104 = 56 + 3y$

"y" is the number of cannonballs Urgum has bought, and as "y" is the only unknown in the equation, Thag should be able to solve it. What Thag needs to do is move the bits of the equation round so that the "y" is all by itself on one side and everything else is on the other, so we can see what "y" is equal to.

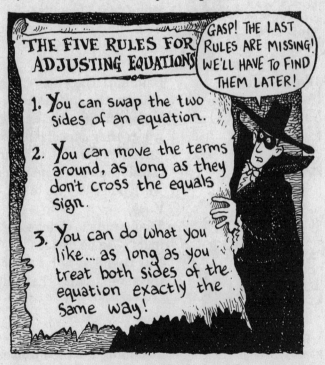

THE FIVE RULES FOR ADJUSTING EQUATIONS

GASP! THE LAST RULES ARE MISSING! WE'LL HAVE TO FIND THEM LATER!

1. You can swap the two sides of an equation.

2. You can move the terms around, as long as they don't cross the equals sign.

3. You can do what you like... as long as you treat both sides of the equation exactly the same way!

(By the way, a **term** is one little bit of an equation, such as + 104, + 56 or + 3y.)

Let's see how Thag works out "y".

$104 = 56 + 3y$	This is what Thag started with.
$56 + 3y = 104$	He's used rule 1 to move the side of the equation with "y" in it to the left.
$3y + 56 = 104$	Using rule 2, he's put the "y" term at the front.
$3y + 56 - 56 = 104 - 56$	Aha! This is clever. Thag wants to get rid of the "+56" on the left-hand side, so using rule 3 he puts "−56" on both sides of the equation.

I'LL SHOW YOU A WAY OF SKIPPING THIS LINE SOON!

$3y = 104 - 56$	Brilliant! Thag has +56 and −56 on the left-hand side, and +56−56 = 0. In other words they cancel out, so he can get rid of both of them...
$3y = 48$	...and then Thag just has to work out 104 − 56 to get 48. Easy!
$3y \div 3 = 48 \div 3$	Thag wants to change $3y$ into just "y" so he divides it by 3. But rule 3 says he must do the same to the other side.

YOU CAN SKIP THIS LINE, TOO!

$y = 48 \div 3$	The $3y$ and the $\div$ 3 cancel to give y...
$y = 16$	And finally that's the answer!

30

Thag can now tell Princess Laplace what she wanted to know.

URGUM HAS BOUGHT 2 CANNONS AND 16 GORESPLATT CANNON-BALLS.

ARGHH! DON'T TELL ME! I DON'T WANT TO KNOW!

As the shop has gone quiet for a moment, we'll look at a few short cuts to use when solving equations...

Crossing the equals sign

When Thag solved his equation, he got from $3y + 56 = 104$ to $3y = 104 - 56$. He did this by putting a step in the middle where he put "−56" on both sides, so that the +56 and −56 would cancel. However, if you're really confident of what you're doing, you can miss this step out. If you want to move a *term* such as "+ 56" across to the other side of an equation, all you need to do is change the sign.

HERE'S HOW IT WORKS...

TO MOVE A TERM ACROSS...

$$3y + 56 = 104$$

MOVE ACROSS AND CHANGE SIGN.

$$3y = 104 - 56$$

CHANGE + TO − OR − TO +

Now we'll try it in different ways with simple numbers so you can check the sums are correct.

Let's start with:
You can move the +1 across and
change the sign to get:
Or, if you wanted, you could move
the 3 across instead and get:

$$3+1=4$$
$$3=4-1$$
$$1=4-3$$

(Notice that the "3" was positive even though the sign wasn't marked, but when it crossed over it changed to negative.)

When you move negative numbers they become positive.

If you start with:
it could become:

$$7-2=5$$
$$7=5+2$$

You can even move everything from one side!

This equation:
could turn into this:
or even this:

$$8-6=2$$
$$8-6-2=0$$
$$0=2+6-8$$

Of course, these rules also work with letters, the only problem is that you can't check the answers like you can with numbers. So make sure you get it right! $a + b = c$ can change to $a = c - b$ or even $a + b - c = 0$.

Remember when Thag had $3y = 48$ and this went to $y = 48 \div 3$? There was a step that showed him dividing both sides by 3, but again if you know what you're doing you don't need it. Thag moved the *coefficient* of y, which was 3. If you imagine the $3y$ as $y \times 3$, when you move the "$\times 3$" to the other side of the equals sign, you just change the sign from $\times$ to $\div$.

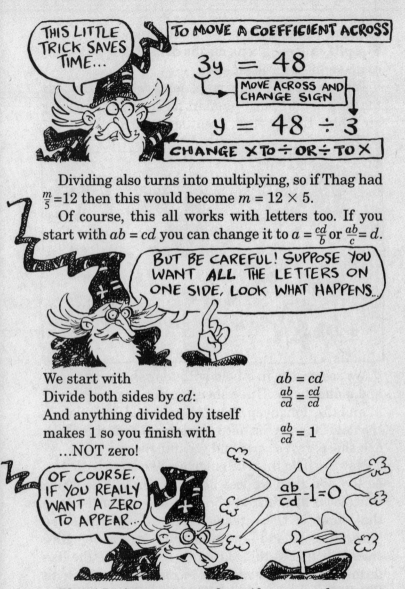

THIS LITTLE TRICK SAVES TIME...

TO MOVE A COEFFICIENT ACROSS

$$3y = 48$$

MOVE ACROSS AND CHANGE SIGN

$$y = 48 \div 3$$

CHANGE × TO ÷ OR ÷ TO ×

Dividing also turns into multiplying, so if Thag had $\frac{m}{5} = 12$ then this would become $m = 12 \times 5$.

Of course, this all works with letters too. If you start with $ab = cd$ you can change it to $a = \frac{cd}{b}$ or $\frac{ab}{c} = d$.

BUT BE CAREFUL! SUPPOSE YOU WANT ALL THE LETTERS ON ONE SIDE, LOOK WHAT HAPPENS...

We start with $ab = cd$

Divide both sides by cd: $\frac{ab}{cd} = \frac{cd}{cd}$

And anything divided by itself
makes 1 so you finish with $\frac{ab}{cd} = 1$

    ...NOT zero!

OF COURSE, IF YOU REALLY WANT A ZERO TO APPEAR...

$$\frac{ab}{cd} - 1 = 0$$

Phew! Let's move on and see if we can take a rest from maths for a minute.

Making life simple

Simplifying equations means doing a few tiny sums to make things look simpler.

But, before we do any more sums, we'll pop outside the back of the Slaught-o-Mart for some fresh country air. Ahhh, that's better. Breathe in deeply now … oh, pooh-ee!

We seem to be in a field with four sheep, five cows and a dungheap. Three sheep go out, two cows come in and the dungheap stays where it is. What's left in the field? It's not too hard to work out that there'll be one sheep, seven cows and the dungheap.

Now we'll do this with algebra. We start with $4s + 5c + d$ and then we lose $3s$ and gain $2c$. The whole thing looks like this: $4s + 5c + d - 3s + 2c$. You'll notice that some of these terms have exactly the same letters (eg $4s$ and $-3s$) and these are called **like terms**. It makes things clearer if you move the like terms together. (Remember to move the signs with them! The minus sign MUST stay with the 3s.) You get: $4s - 3s + 5c + 2c + d$.

When you simplify, you just add or subtract like terms, so $4s - 3s$ becomes $1s$. But, nobody bothers putting the "1" in so we just put "s". $5c + 2c$ becomes $7c$. The dungheap doesn't have any other dungheaps wandering in to join it, so it just stays where it is. You finish with $s + 7c + d$.

What you can't do is add or subtract *unlike* terms. Suppose your field just has eight pigs and a dungheap. You can't take away four chickens because there aren't any. If you made this into an equation you'd have $8p - 4c + d$ and you can't do much apart from try to stop the pigs rolling in the dungheap and accidentally squashing the negative chickens that aren't there.

But hang on, what's this? It seems that another little dungheap *has* wandered into the field...

And so Hunjah the Headless steps out of his costume and sneaks into the Slaught-o-Mart. He is a worried man – and with good reason. His little yak-

35

skin tent is pitched right beside the crossroads where the tracks from the other barbarians' caves meet up. He'd like to move the tent, but sadly he's not strong enough to pull the pegs out. And now that Urgum, Mungoid and Grizelda have stocked up with weapons, it's very likely they'll take a pop at each other and he'll be caught right in the middle. Of course, he *could* rely on Captain Cancel to keep the peace...

...but maybe not. Hunjah hurries over to the plasters, pills and potions department and plans to spend everything he has. Despite the lack of sharp and explosive things, this is by far the spookiest corner of the Slaught-o-Mart. As Hunjah is waiting for the healthwitch to appear, he can't resist slipping a two groat piece into the "I Speak Your Fate" machine.

At last, the healthwitch comes through. She has just brewed up a new potion, Magic Wound Glue, which sounds essential to Hunjah. It has an interesting price though...

Because he's already spent two groats, Hunjah can only afford one tube of the glue. He decides to spend everything else he has on six nettleleaf plasters, and each plaster costs 17 groats less than the Magic Wound Glue.

I NEED TO KNOW HOW MUCH MONEY HUNJAH HAD TO START WITH.

Amazingly enough, we can work it out. We'll call Hunjah's money H.

First of all, we need to work out an **expression** to show what the magic glue cost. (An expression is a little bunch of numbers and letters that describe something.) As the tube cost half what Hunjah brought into the shop, we can describe the cost as $\frac{H}{2}$.

The plasters each cost 17 groats less than a tube of glue, so we can make another expression to describe the cost of each plaster: $(\frac{H}{2} - 17)$. You'll notice we put it in brackets to make sure the bits stay together. This way we can quickly say that six plasters cost $6(\frac{H}{2} - 17)$.

So when Hunjah bought his magic glue and the six plasters, in total he spent:

$$\frac{H}{2} + 6(\frac{H}{2} - 17)$$

But how much money did he have when he approached the counter? He walked into the shop with H, but he put two groats in the machine! Therefore when he got to the counter he only had $(H - 2)$ groats left and that's how much he paid to the healthwitch. So the final equation is:

$$(H - 2) = \frac{H}{2} + 6\left(\frac{H}{2} - 17\right)$$

It looks nasty, but as there's only one unknown we should be able to find what Hunjah started with. The trick is to do all the jobs in the right order:

- simplify anything in the brackets;
- multiply out the brackets;
- move the like terms together (and try to get all the unknowns on the left-hand side);
- simplify whatever you can;
- do whatever it takes to leave "H" by itself on the left-hand side.

$(H - 2) = \frac{H}{2} + 6(\frac{H}{2} - 17)$ To start with, see if anything

in the brackets will simplify ... sadly, they won't. Next, we multiply out the brackets. As the $(H - 2)$ bracket doesn't have a coefficient marked, we can assume the coefficient is +1 which means that we can just take those brackets away. The other bracket has a coefficient of +6, so we multiply both the $\frac{H}{2}$ and the −17 by +6.

$H - 2 = \frac{H}{2} + \frac{6H}{2} - 102$ It's a bit of a mess, but let's move all the "H" bits to one side and all the other numbers to the other side.

REMEMBER TO CHANGE THE SIGN ON ANY TERM THAT CHANGES SIDES!

39

$H - \frac{H}{2} - \frac{6H}{2} = -102 + 2$ Those 2s under the H terms are a bit depressing so let's multiply everything on both sides by 2 to get rid of them.

$2 \times H - 2 \times \frac{H}{2} - 2 \times \frac{6H}{2}$ $= -102 \times 2 + 2 \times 2$ This a really neat move. If you look at the fractions, they all have a 2 on top and a 2 on the bottom. Therefore these 2s cancel out which makes life so much easier.

$2H - H - 6H = -204 + 4$ Wahey – the fractions have gone! Now we can simplify the like terms.

$-5H = -200$ Now it doesn't look so bad. It's just a shame about the negative signs. But suppose we multiply both sides by –1?

$5H = 200$ Oh yes, indeedy, that's much better! Finally, we divide both sides by 5 to get:

$H = 40$

SO HUNJAH STARTED WITH 40 GROATS.

It looks like a lot of work, but that's because we've taken you through it in tiny steps to make sure you understand. If you're feeling really keen, you could also work out that the Magic Wound Glue cost 20 groats and each nettleleaf plaster cost three groats, but you've had a long tough chapter, so let's move on.

41

THE FATHER OF ALGEBRA

If you've got this far in the book – well done! The last chapter has explained all the basics of algebra that would take normal people YEARS to learn. You've done it in 23 pages. So let's take a minute to meet the bloke who was supposed to have invented the sort of algebra we know today.

Back in the time of ancient Greece, people loved playing with puzzles like "can you find a number that you can cube and then add one to which then equals another number squared?" It's hard enough to understand the question, never mind trying to get the answer! Luckily it looks a lot clearer if you write it out like this: $p^3 + 1 = q^2$

All you've got to do is find whole numbers for p and q. Even if you can't solve the problem, at least the letters and signs make it fairly obvious what you're being asked to do.*

The idea of using letters and other symbols in maths problems was developed by Diophantus – a Greek mathematician who lived in Alexandria, Egypt. The funny thing about Diophantus is that although we're not sure when he was alive (it was some time between 200 and 300 AD) we do know exactly how long he lived for. One of

* Answer: the only whole numbers that work are p = 2 and q = 3.

his fans described his life with the sort of puzzle that the Greek would have appreciated:

DIOPHANTUS' YOUTH LASTED ONE-SIXTH OF HIS LIFE. HE GREW A BEARD AFTER ONE-TWELFTH MORE OF HIS LIFE, THEN AFTER ONE-SEVENTH MORE, DIOPHANTUS MARRIED. FIVE YEARS LATER HE HAD A SON WHO LIVED EXACTLY HALF AS LONG AS HIS FATHER. DIOPHANTUS DIED FOUR YEARS AFTER HIS SON.

So what does this tell us?

IF YOU WANT TO GET MARRIED, GROW A BEARD!

YUK!

Er … no. The puzzle tells us how long Diophantus lived, but the only chance we've got to solve it is to turn all the information into an equation.

Let's say that the number of years he lived was D.

His youth was one-sixth of his life so we can write that as: $\frac{D}{6}$

It was another one-twelfth of his life before the beard so that's: $\frac{D}{12}$

Then another one-seventh before he married: $\frac{D}{7}$

Then it was five years before his son was born: 5

The son lived exactly half as long as Diophantus: $\frac{D}{2}$

And then there was another four years at the end: 4

43

If you add all these bits up, you get Diophantus's total age, which all the way along we've called D. So we can write this as an equation:

$$\frac{D}{6} + \frac{D}{12} + \frac{D}{7} + 5 + \frac{D}{2} + 4 = D$$

Look at all those numbers on the bottom. Urgh!

If you've read *The Mean and Vulgar Bits* you'll be keen to work out the LCD of 6, 12, 7 and 2, and then multiply it by everything in sight. But if you haven't read *M and V* don't worry. We're going to charge in headfirst using a deadly combination of muscle and attitude.

For an equation like this, find the biggest number on the bottom and multiply EVERYTHING by it. The biggest number is 12, so here we go:

$$2D + D + \frac{12D}{7} + 60 + 6D + 48 = 12D$$

Not bad. Just about everything cancelled (for example the first term became $\frac{12 \times D}{6}$ which cancelled to make $2D$) but we're still left with a rather ugly $\frac{12D}{7}$ fraction. In a minute, we'll multiply everything by 7 to get rid of it, but to save ourselves a lot of effort, we'll simplify things first. If we organize the left-hand side we get:

$$2D + D + 6D + \frac{12D}{7} + 60 + 48 = 12D$$

$$9D + \frac{12D}{7} + 108 = 12D$$

And we'll move the D terms to one side:

$$108 = 12D - 9D - \frac{12D}{7}$$

And that becomes $108 = 3D - \frac{12D}{7}$.

Now we've only got three terms left, so to get rid of the fraction we'll multiply them all by 7.

$756 = 21D - 12D$ We're getting there...

$756 = 9D$

Swap the sides and divide both through by 9 to get:

$D = 84$.

Phew!

So Diophantus lived for 84 years, which was a long time for those days. Who'd have thought that algebra was so good for you?

An expensive mistake

When you treat both sides of an equation the same way, you must think it through carefully. For instance, if there are 100 pennies in £1 you could put £1 = 100p. But what happens if you square both sides of this equation? You get $(£1)^2 = (100p)^2$ and that becomes £1 = 10,000p. But surely 10,000p = £100 and not £1? What's gone wrong?

I'VE FOUND ONE OF THE MISSING RULES FROM PAGE 29!

4. Avoid using different units in an equation.

This rule will avoid expensive mistakes like this! If you're playing around with money equations, don't have pounds on one side and pence on the other.

How did algebra get called algebra?

Long after Diophantus lived his 84 years, algebra was making big advances in the Arab world, where it was called "restoration and balancing". Around 1,200 years ago, there was a brilliant mathematician and astronomer called Al-Khwarizmi who really pushed things forward. He was the first person to call equations and letters and signs "al-jabru" – the Arab word for "restoration". So now you know.

By the way, "bananas" are named after the Arab word "banan", which means "finger". Be honest, we pack a terrific range of facts into these books, don't we?

PACKING, UNPACKING AND THE PANIC BUTTON

It's all joy and excitement at Fogsworth Manor because it's the time of year when the cream of society takes a well-earned break from the tedious circuit of garden parties, opera nights, film premiers and polo tournaments. At last they can whisk themselves off to the coast for a couple of days and luxuriate amid the opulence and splendour of Brownpool-on-Sea.

Let's see how Primrose Poppet is getting on with her packing.

Sometimes packing is so simple – and it can be the same with maths. Look at these loose terms here:

$$6p^2 - 8p + 12dp$$

Let's **factorize** them, which means packing them as neatly as we can into a bracket. The trick is to see if there's anything that will divide into all the terms. Here we find that we can divide everything by 2, and this is so tempting that we simply cannot resist. Once we've divided each term by 2 we put the results inside a bracket and put 2 outside. We get: $2(3p^2 - 4p + 6dp)$

If you look at the terms in the brackets you can see that they all have at least one "p" as well, so let's tidy that up: $2p(3p - 4 + 6d)$

As there's nothing else that will divide into all the terms, that's about it. Obviously, **expanding** (in other words unpacking) the bracket is easy! Just multiply everything inside the bracket by the $2p$ outside the bracket:

$$2p(3p - 4 + 6d) = 2p \times 3p - 2p \times 4 + 2p \times 6d$$
$$= 6p^2 - 8p + 12dp$$

Life with one bracket is a bit like travelling with one suitcase. Packing is as simple as unpacking, unless you do a bit of shopping while you're away... In that case, packing can be trickier.

If you've got to deal with two suitcases, then things are rather different. At least unpacking is always quite simple, as we'll see when the Duchess and the Colonel arrive at the guest house:

Unpacking a pair of brackets is just as easy. Look at these: $(f + 2)(f + 5)$

Aren't they neat? Two brackets next to each other like this means you have to multiply them together so you need to work out $(f + 2) \times (f + 5)$. You have to make sure that everything in the first bracket is multiplied by everything in the second bracket. Here's the safest way of doing it:

- Open the first bracket to get the "f" and the "+ 2" out. You then multiply both these bits by the second bracket. It should look like this:
  $f(f + 5) + 2(f + 5)$
- Multiply out the brackets: $f^2 + 5f + 2f + 10$
- Simplify the like terms. Here, the like terms are $+ 5f$ and $+ 2f$, so we end up with $f^2 + 7f + 10$

No big problems there, but the fun part comes when you want to pack it all up again. You could try and find something that will divide into all three terms of $f^2 + 7f + 10$, but you won't have much luck. The best you can do is $f(f + 7) + 10$ which is a bit depressing. If this thing is going to pack up at all, you'll need two brackets. That brings us to the problems of two suitcases...

51

The hardest part of packing two suitcases is sorting out exactly which items should go in which case. Strangely enough, it's the same problem with packing two brackets.

Quadratics

There's a special expression that always needs two brackets when you want to pack it away. It's called a **quadratic** and it has three bits: a squared term, a linear (or middle) term and a constant. Our $f^2 + 7f + 10$ expression is a quadratic and we need to examine it for clues to tell us what to do.

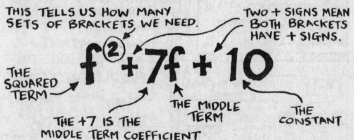

THIS TELLS US HOW MANY SETS OF BRACKETS WE NEED.

TWO + SIGNS MEAN BOTH BRACKETS HAVE + SIGNS.

$$f^{(2)} + 7f + 10$$

THE SQUARED TERM

THE +7 IS THE MIDDLE TERM COEFFICIENT

THE MIDDLE TERM

THE CONSTANT

We know we'll need two sets of brackets, so we may as well draw them in before we start. (   )(   )

Quadratics always end up with one unknown letter in each bracket. As our unknown is f, we can put one in each bracket. (f)(f)

Now it's time to activate a special new invention…

THE MURDEROUS MATHS
QUADRATIC CRACKER
PATENT PENDING   ALL RIGHTS RESERVED

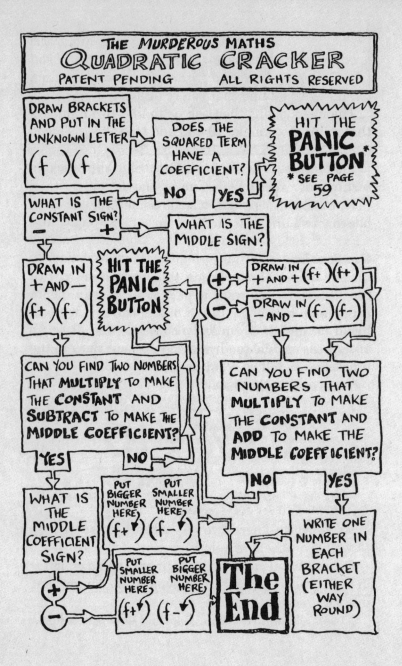

DRAW BRACKETS AND PUT IN THE UNKNOWN LETTER

$(f \quad)(f \quad)$

DOES THE SQUARED TERM HAVE A COEFFICIENT?

NO   YES

HIT THE **PANIC BUTTON** *
* SEE PAGE 59

WHAT IS THE CONSTANT SIGN?
−   +

WHAT IS THE MIDDLE SIGN?

DRAW IN + AND −
$(f+)(f-)$

HIT THE **PANIC BUTTON**

+
−

DRAW IN + AND + $(f+)(f+)$

DRAW IN − AND − $(f-)(f-)$

CAN YOU FIND TWO NUMBERS THAT **MULTIPLY** TO MAKE THE **CONSTANT** AND **SUBTRACT** TO MAKE THE **MIDDLE COEFFICIENT?**

YES   NO

CAN YOU FIND TWO NUMBERS THAT **MULTIPLY** TO MAKE THE **CONSTANT** AND **ADD** TO MAKE THE **MIDDLE COEFFICIENT?**

NO   YES

WHAT IS THE MIDDLE COEFFICIENT SIGN?

PUT BIGGER NUMBER HERE↴ PUT SMALLER NUMBER HERE↴
$(f+\,)\,(f-\,)$

WRITE ONE NUMBER IN EACH BRACKET (EITHER WAY ROUND)

+
−

PUT SMALLER NUMBER HERE↴ PUT BIGGER NUMBER HERE↴
$(f+\,)\,(f-\,)$

The End

54

Thanks to our modern technology the quadratic drudgery of the past is now a pleasant pastime. If you take $f^2 + 7f + 10$ and put it through the cracker, in a twinkling you'll find that you've drawn $(f +)(f +)$.

The instructions then ask us to find two numbers that multiply to make 10 and add to make 7. This is simple because $5 \times 2 = 10$ and $5 + 2 = 7$. Once you've found these numbers, you plonk them in the brackets and bingo… $(f + 2)(f + 5)$ That's the answer.

Now let's try cracking an expression that we *don't* know: $g^2 + 4g - 21$. Using the cracker we quickly find we've written $(g +)(g -)$. This time, we need two numbers that multiply to make 21 and subtract to make 4. (Note: the cracker deals automatically with the coefficient and constant signs, so you can ignore the minus in front of the 21.) The only numbers to make 21 are 7×3, and luckily $7 - 3 = 4$ so there we are! As the middle coefficient is +, we put the 7 in the bracket with +. The result is $(g + 7)(g - 3)$.

Try cracking these yourself:

$h^2 - 6h - 27$ $\qquad$ $j^2 - 4j + 3$ $\qquad$ $k^2 + 14k - 32$

Did you get any of these answers right? If so, then your packing is certainly better than Croak's was…

When one equation has two answers

Before we go on, we thought you'd like to see what happened in the boardroom at the Murderous Maths headquarters when the executive directors first saw this section of the book.

Yes, the next bit is tough but regular Murderous Maths readers will know why it's been included. Even if you don't quite follow it, fold the book open on these pages and then casually drop it in front of somebody. When they pick it up and see that you've been reading about quadratic equations, they will think you are utterly brilliant. You'll get top credibility points at no personal expense – and not many books can do that for you.

Quadratics usually turn up in equations that have a zero on the right-hand side like this: $f^2 + 7f + 10 = 0$

In case you're wondering, this sort of equation comes up when you're firing things into the air and wondering where they will land. You'll get an idea of how they work on page 140.

Although there is a squared term, quadratic equations only have one unknown so we should be able to solve them. The exciting part is that they have *two* possible answers! In other words, there are two different numbers that f can be and the equation will still work. The way to find the two answers of $f^2 + 7f + 10 = 0$ is to factorize the left-hand side to get this: $(f + 5)(f + 2) = 0$

Now think to yourself … *anything multiplied by zero makes zero!* So if the first bracket worked out to be zero, it wouldn't matter what the second bracket worked out to be – the answer would still be zero. So, the equation would work! The question is: what does "f" have to equal to make the value of the first bracket zero? We can make this into a little equation: $f + 5 = 0$, from which we get $f = -5$. Now we can see if this value works in our complete equation.

Start with $f^2 + 7f + 10 = 0$, then swap f for –5: $(-5)^2 + 7 \times -5 + 10 = 0$

58

REMEMBER THAT MINUS × MINUS = PLUS!

25 − 35 + 10 = 0 It works!

However suppose the *second* bracket was zero. It wouldn't matter what the first bracket was. In this case, $f + 2 = 0$, so $f = -2$. Let's try it:

$(-2)^2 + 7 \times -2 + 10 = 0$

$4 - 14 + 10 = 0$

It works again!

So, the two solutions for this equation are $f = -5$ *or* -2!

The PANIC button

Sometimes, our quadratic cracker won't give an answer and it's for one of two reasons.

- The squared term has a coefficient (other than + 1) e.g. $12m^2 - 7m - 10 = 0$. If you have a super maths brain you might be able to deal with this and get $(4m - 5)(3m + 2) = 0$ and then get $m = \frac{5}{4}$ *or* $-\frac{2}{3}$, but let's pretend that you haven't. Although the cracker will help you put the right signs in, getting all the numbers in the brackets is a tricky business.

- You try as hard as you can, but you can't think of any numbers that will fit in the bracket. That's because sometimes there aren't any whole numbers that will give an answer!

If you get stuck like this, you have to reach under your desk and push the secret PANIC BUTTON.

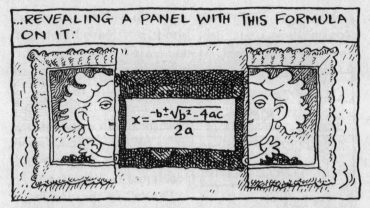

...REVEALING A PANEL WITH THIS FORMULA ON IT:

$$x = \frac{-b \pm \sqrt{b^2 - 4ac}}{2a}$$

This formula can solve any quadratic equation. The clever bit is the ± sign which means *plus OR minus*. The way you get the two answers is to treat this superstar formula like *two* formulas, one with a "+" and one with a "–" like this:

$$x = \frac{-b + \sqrt{b^2 - 4ac}}{2a} \text{ or } x = \frac{-b - \sqrt{b^2 - 4ac}}{2a}$$

THIS IS ONE VERY AWESOME WEAPON. IT LOOKS NASTY, BUT JUST RELAX AND LET IT DO THE HARD WORK FOR YOU!

By the way, you DO have a panic button under your desk, don't you? No? Oh, dear... It's absolutely vital to have one! As you're one of our valued Murderous Maths readers, we'll send round a trusted panic-button installer to sort you out.

DING DONG

MM PANIC-BUTTON INSTALLER

That'll be him now, so let him in and leave him to get on with it. In the meantime, here's how to use the formula.

You have to imagine that your problem equation is $ax^2 + bx + c = 0$ so let's see how it works with our old problem: $f^2 + 7f + 10 = 0$.

The "x" is the unknown bit of your equation so we just swap "x" for "f" in the formula. The coefficients "a," "b" and "c" are more important. "a" is the coefficient of the f^2 so $a = +1$. "b" is the coefficient of the middle term so $b = +7$. "c" is the constant at the end, so $c = +10$. We put these values into the formulas.

❌ **WARNING! Here's where nearly everybody gets the formula wrong. Remember that the first bit of the formula is "–b", so don't forget to put that minus sign in!**

On we go...

$$f = \frac{-7 + \sqrt{7^2 - 4 \times 1 \times 10}}{2 \times 1} \text{ or } \frac{-7 - \sqrt{7^2 - 4 \times 1 \times 10}}{2 \times 1}$$

Ahh! It's always a bit of a relief to get the numbers in, isn't it? Before we go on, we'll just check and see how your new panic button is coming along.

Everything seems fine, so let's crumble those numbers. Do the bit inside that square-root sign first...

$$f = \frac{-7 + \sqrt{49 - 40}}{2} \text{ or } \frac{-7 - \sqrt{49 - 40}}{2}$$

$$f = \frac{-7 + \sqrt{9}}{2} \text{ or } \frac{-7 - \sqrt{9}}{2}$$

$$f = \frac{-7 + 3}{2} \text{ or } \frac{-7 - 3}{2}$$

$$f = \frac{-4}{2} \text{ or } \frac{-10}{2}$$

And that gives the same answers that we worked out before: $f = -2$ *or* -5.

That's the portrait of your Great-great-aunt Marina going up, so while it's being wired in we'll try the formula on a *real stinker:* $12m^2 - 7m - 10 = 0$

In our formula $a = +12$, $b = -7$ and $c = -10$, so let's put them in:

$$m = \frac{+7 \pm \sqrt{(-7)^2 - 4 \times 12 \times -10}}{2 \times 12}$$

We've left the $\pm$ sign in for now, we can wait a minute before we split it into $+$ and $-$. Also you'll see that where the "$-b$" goes we've put "$+7$." That's because $b = -7$ and so $-b = -(-7)$, which is $+7$. You really have to watch these sneaky $+$ and $-$ signs. Let's bash the numbers out now…

$$m = \frac{+7 \pm \sqrt{49 + 480}}{24} = \frac{+7 \pm \sqrt{529}}{24} = \frac{+7 \pm 23}{24}$$

Now we'll split the $\pm$ sign into $+$ and $-$ so we get two answers:

$$m = \frac{+7 + 23}{24} \ \ or \ \ \frac{+7 - 23}{24}$$

$$m = \frac{30}{24} = \frac{5}{4} \ \ or \ \ \frac{-16}{24} = -\frac{2}{3}$$

So the two answers to $12m^2 - 7m - 10 = 0$ turn out to be $m = \frac{5}{4} \ or - \frac{2}{3}$.

(You usually get fraction answers when the squared term has a coefficient.)

Is that tough enough for you…?

At last! Your panic button is being fitted, so there are just a few final connections to go and it'll be ready. Exciting, eh? You'll be surprised at how often you need it, because

sometimes quadratic equations give answers that are even uglier than the fractions we've just seen.

Ugly answers

If you look at the quadratic formula there's a bit where you have to work out $\sqrt{b^2 - 4ac}$. This is fine if the value of b^2 is bigger than the value of $4ac$ but suppose your equation is $5x^2 + 4x + 4$? This means you get $a = +5$ and $b = +4$ and $c = +4$, so inside the bracket you'll get $\sqrt{16 - 80}$ which is $\sqrt{-64}$. This is the sort of spooky thing that makes all the lights flicker and the cat climb up inside the chimney, because you need *the square root of a negative number*. The answer to $\sqrt{-64}$ isn't +8 because $(+8)^2 = +64$. And the answer isn't –8 either because $(-8)^2$ *also* makes +64.

There *is* an answer, but we have to abandon normal numbers: $\sqrt{-64} = \pm 8i$. The little "i" is the *imaginary* number that represents $\sqrt{-1}$. We're not going to worry about that now, but if you'd like to know more about "i" it's explained in *Numbers: The Key to the Universe*.

By the way, if you go on to finish this equation, you get the two answers: $x = \frac{-4 \pm 8i}{10}$ so $x = \frac{2+4i}{5}$ or $\frac{2-4i}{5}$. Happy now?

HELLO!

(If you're a pure mathematician looking for an extra thrill, you could go on to factorize the tops and get $x = \frac{2(1 + 2i)}{5}$ or $\frac{2(1 - 2i)}{5}$. For some people, the fun just never stops...)

The good news is that when you're working out what a few sweets cost, or when you're measuring your ceiling to fit a carpet in case gravity suddenly starts working upside-down, you'll never need sums like this. The big secret of sums like this isn't how to solve them, it's how to AVOID them!

Great! The technician has just about finished and what a good job he's done. As soon as he's gone, you can try your new panic button, but first look at these two equations:

$$x^2 - x + 12 = 0 \qquad x^2 - x - 12 = 0$$

To the untrained eye, they look almost the same, but one is deadly simple and the other is simply deadly! Which is which?

Answer: $x^2 - x - 12 = 0$ is simple!
It works out to $(x + 3)(x - 4) = 0$ so x can be $+4$ or -3.
But $x^2 - x + 12 = 0$ is deadly...
The two answers for x are $\frac{1 + 6.856i}{2}$ and $\frac{1 - 6.856i}{2}$.

No living soul should ever have to contemplate the horrific implications of such answers. Mind you, some living souls DO contemplate them – some even enjoy it!

You can find other methods of solving quadratic equations (there's even a special quadratic calculator) at www.murderousmaths.co.uk

Maybe you find it hard to believe that two almost identical equations could have such different answers? Would you like to check? Then go on, you know you want to … push your brand new PANIC BUTTON!

Oh no – it's your arch enemy Professor Fiendish with yet another diabolical challenge! He must have been disguised as the Murderous Maths technician and instead of a panic button he installed a "Summon the Professor" button under your desk. Time to be cool.

"So," you say. "I suppose that was you crawling about the room fixing wires and motors on everything?"

"Indeed," cackles the Professor. "And you never suspected. And now you've let me in with another diabolical challenge."

"Let me get this right," you say. "You came in here before and slaved away for hours hammering, drilling and even sweeping up?"

"Yes," he says proudly.

"Just so you could come in AGAIN and give me a diabolical challenge?"

"That's it."

"Why didn't you just give me the challenge in the first place, and not bother with all the building work?"

"Because..." falters the Professor. He hadn't thought of that. In desperation he waves a flimsy slip of paper under your nose. "You might be laughing now, but you just wait! You think you know about equations, do you? Well, see what you make of *this* one!"

$$(9+Z)(1+Z) = 6 + 7Z + Z^2$$

"You're not having a good day, are you?" you say after a quick glance. "Even your little sum is wrong. If you multiply out the brackets you get $9 + 10Z + Z^2$. It's easy."

"I KNOW it's wrong!" screams the Professor. "It's supposed to be wrong, that's the challenge! You must alter this equation so that it DOES work. Otherwise the next time I turn up and do hours of unnecessary building work, *I won't hoover up afterwards!*"

What a ghastly thought, you think, as a bead of yellow sweat drips off the Professor's nose and splatters on to your desk. Fancy having him in your house and not having it cleaned straight away!

"That should be simple enough," you say, reaching for a pencil.

"Hang on!" the Professor says as his cold clammy hand grasps your wrist. It feels like being licked by a giant sea slug. "You haven't heard the diabolical bit yet!"

YOU ARE **NOT** ALLOWED TO WRITE ANYTHING DOWN OR RUB ANYTHING OUT!

Diabolical indeed. There's only one thing for it — you'll have to copy the equation out of this book on to a slip of paper yourself and see if you can beat the Professor's challenge!

Meanwhile, the Professor is strutting around and looking unbearably pleased with himself.

"Har har!" he snarls. "You can't comprehend how unbearably pleased with myself I am. You think you can deal with a bit of Murderous Maths, do you? Well, you can't! Your quadratic formula isn't much help to you now, is it? No, and do you know why? Because it's pathetic…"

You let him ramble on because of course he has no idea that under the desk you have been quietly undoing the cover of the panic button. Ping! Off it comes. With amazing dexterity, you reach inside and reverse the wires.

"Well?" he says. "Admit it. Your formula is totally USELESS! What do you say to *that*?"

"I've just got one thing to say," you say in a just-got-one-thingish sort of way.

"And what might that be?" enquires the Professor.

"Goodbye!"

You push the button. The reversed connection sucks the Professor back into the wall behind the portrait of Great-great-aunt Marina which snaps shut. There's no sign of the Professor apart from the fact that Great-great-aunt Marina seems to have acquired a real nose. What's worse, it's dripping…

Oh well, that's all part of the rich tapestry of life that is Murderous Maths.

Even tougher equations

I'VE ADDED IN THIS SECTION JUST FOR YOU...

You have just got through the toughest part of the book, but I know what Murderous Maths readers are like. Dealing with x^2 equations wasn't hard enough for you, was it? You want MORE, don't you? You're desperate to take on higher powers such as x^3 or x^4 or even ... x^5, aren't you?

Well sorry, but quadratic combat is as far as I dare to take you. I know you're upset so I'd like to spend a few moments explaining why. Be warned though, this is top-level highly restricted information which has never before been revealed... So, in case anybody is watching you, follow my ((special instructions)) so that they don't suspect.

IS ANYONE TAKING TOO MUCH INTEREST IN WHAT YOU'RE READING RIGHT NOW? NO? GOOD. THEN READ ON...

Mathematicians have known ways to attack and beat quadratic equations for thousands of years, even though many of them didn't understand the idea of negative numbers or the number zero. (And speaking of zero, soon you'll see how zero is the biggest threat to the existence of the universe.) ((Smile to yourself and scratch your nose.))

But there are lots of equations that are even worse than quadratics! Cubic equations have an x^3 term such as $x^3 - 4x^2 - 9x + 7 = 0$. There was no obvious way of solving cubics until the 16th century, when an Italian mathematician, Scipione del Ferro, suggested a method that was further developed by Niccolò Tartaglia. ((Quick! In case somebody is passing by you must laugh out loud. If anyone asks, say you think Tartaglia sounds funny, ha ha ha.))

This method was stolen by Gerolamo Cardano who was as well known for his gambling and violence as for his maths. A pupil of Cardano's called Ludovico Ferrari went on to solve quartic equations, which included an x^4 term.

After that, mathematicians tried to deal with equations with an x^5 term until it was proved that finding the solutions was usually impossible. Even though we know the answers are roaming around out there, actually grabbing hold of them is a different matter. ((One final big laugh, wipe eyes and regain your composure. Nobody will suspect that this isn't funny but deadly serious.))

So there you have it. Anything much tougher than a quadratic is probably impossible. And, by the way, Gerolamo was secretly known as the Phantom G, and Ludovico was the Phantom L. They were two of the best agents in the field.

And, I may as well tell you one last secret. The reason I'm known as the Phantom X is because my first name is Xylophone.

OK, YOU'VE DONE THE HARD WORK!

NOW TURN THE PAGE FOR SOME FUN!

Diabolical answer... Tear the paper just before the equals sign, then turn the left-hand side upside down! You get:

$$(z+1)(z+6) = 6 + 7z + z^2$$

THE MECHANICS OF MAGIC

One of the best things about maths is that there are tonnes of magic-number tricks you can do. Even when you know how to do them, it's quite a mystery why they work until you try them out with a bit of algebra.

The 22 trick

Here's a great trick to play on a friend called Mavis (but DON'T tell her that this is called the "22" trick). All you need is:

● a pencil;
● some paper;
● an aerobatic stunt pilot.

Before you start, you need to have a quiet word with the pilot.

You then need to pass Mavis a pencil and paper.

Here's what Mavis has to do.
- Write down any three different digits from 1 to 9. (e.g. 291)
- Use the digits to make all the six possible two-digit numbers and add them up.
  (Make SURE Mavis has all six numbers and that none of them are the same.)

- Then Mavis should add together the three digits she chose to start with and divide her answer by the total. (2 + 9 + 1= 12 then finally 264 ÷ 12 = **22**)
- Look out of the window!

Mavis can't fail to be impressed!

The clever bit about the trick is that it doesn't matter which three different digits Mavis chooses, the answer will always be 22.

If you can't arrange a plane, here are some other ways you could reveal the number 22 to Mavis at the end:

It is a great trick, but how does it work?

To start with Mavis has to choose Three Different Numbers, but as we're going to explain this with algebra we'll use the letters $T\ D\ N$. We can arrange these letters to make up the six different two digit "numbers": $TD\ DT\ DN\ ND\ TN\ NT$

Now we add them up, and the secret is to add the tens column and the units column separately.

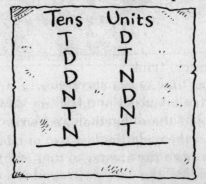

If you count up the letters in the UNITS column, you'll find each letter appears twice, so we get $2T + 2D + 2N$, which we can factorize to make $2(T + D + N)$.

If you count up the letters in the TENS column, again each letter appears twice, so again we finish with $2(T + D + N)$. As this is the tens column, this total equals $2(T + D + N) \times 10$ or $20(T + D + N)$.

Putting together the total of tens and units we get:
$20(T + D + N) + 2(T + D + N)$

We can write this as:
$(20 + 2)(T + D + N) = 22(T + D + N)$.

Now for the last bit of the trick. We add up the three digits, which makes $(T + D + N)$, and divide this into the answer. Easy!

$22(T + D + N) \div (T + D + N) = 22$

There! All the letters disappear and the answer comes out as 22. So it doesn't matter which three digits Mavis chooses to start with. The answer will always be 22.

BUT HOW DID YOU REALLY DO IT?

The Fibonacci trick

In *Numbers: the Key to the Universe*, we saw the Fibonacci trick: you write down any two numbers, and then add them together and write down the answer. You then add the last two numbers of your sum, write down the answer to that and keep going (always adding the last two numbers you wrote down). When you've written down six numbers altogether you stop, then add them all up.

If you started by writing 7 and 4, the line of six numbers would be: 7 4 11 15 26 41

When you add them all up you get 104.

Here's the odd bit: if you get somebody else to write down six numbers like this, you can work out the total before they've even written down the sixth number! All you do is look at the fifth number and multiply it by 4. In the above example, you'll see that the fifth number is 26 and $26 \times 4 = 104$. It doesn't matter which two numbers the line starts with, this always works, and algebra can show us why.

Let's say the two Starting Numbers are S and N. See what you get when you keep adding the last two numbers together (it's easier to keep the Ss and Ns in different columns so we can add them up quickly):

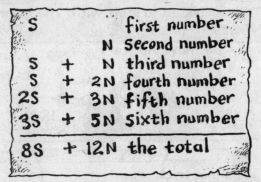

S			first number
		N	second number
S	+	N	third number
S	+	2N	fourth number
2S	+	3N	fifth number
3S	+	5N	sixth number
8S	+	12N	the total

You can see the fifth number is $2S + 3N$. If you multiply this by 4 you get $8S + 12N$ ... which is the total. It doesn't matter what S or N are, and therefore it doesn't matter which two numbers you start with.

Think of a number...
There are hundreds of tricks that start by asking someone to "think of a number"! They can all be explained with a bit of algebra, but what's even more fun is that when you see how they work, you can invent your own. Here's a simple one to give you the idea. Grab Mavis and try this:

THE SECRET: the answer Mavis gives you should end in "0". (If it doesn't then she's gone wrong!) All you do is knock off the zero and subtract 5. So, 180 turns into 18. Subtract 5. The answer is 13! That gives you the number she started with. But why?

Let's say the number Mavis thinks of is m. Here's what happens with the trick:

Think of a number $= m$

Add 2 $= m + 2$

Multiply by 5 $= 5(m + 2)$ $=$ $5m + 10$

Add 15 $= 5m + 10 + 15 =$ $5m + 25$

Multiply by 2 $= 2(5m + 25)$ $=$ $10m + 50$

This is the answer Mavis gives you, and here's what you do in your head:

Take off the zero (i.e. divide by 10) = $m + 5$
Subtract 5   = m

And so you've worked out Mavis's number!

If Mavis picked 27, the different steps would produce the answers: 27, 29, 145, 160 and finally 320. So off goes the "0" to get 32 and then when 5 is subtracted it gives 27 again. It's easy peasy, so why not test this yourself right now. Pick any number you like and try it out!

A bit of advice: when you're performing a number trick, most people are more impressed if the number is linked with something else. If you want this trick to look posher, then instead of asking Mavis to "think of a number" you can ask her to do one of these things instead:

ASK HER TO THROW ONE DIE OR A COUPLE OF DICE AND COUNT THE SPOTS WITHOUT YOU SEEING.

ASK HER TO PICK TWO CARDS FROM A PACK AND ADD UP THEIR VALUES (PICTURE CARDS COUNT AS TEN).

ASK HER HOW MANY TEDDIES SHE HAS IN HER BEDROOM.

ASK HER HOW MANY COINS SHE HAS IN HER PURSE OR POCKET.

The magic card

- Get Mavis to secretly pick any playing card from a pack (apart from a joker).
- Ask her to multiply the number on the card by 5 (jack = 11, queen = 12, king = 13).
- Then if the card is red she should add 20. If it's black add 21.
- Next multiply by 2.
- Finally if the card is a heart or a spade, add 1.
- Mavis tells you her answer and you can tell her what the card is!

THE SECRET! To tell the card's suit, check the last digit: 0 = diamond, 1 = heart, 2 = club, 3 = spade. To tell the number, ignore the last digit and subtract 4. Therefore, if Mavis says 93, the "3" tells you it's spades, and if you work out 9 − 4 her card is the 5 of spades. 160 is the queen of diamonds, 51 is the ace of hearts, 112 is the seven of clubs and so on.

How does it work?
The sums deal with the number of the card and the suit separately. It does this by sneakily multiplying the number of the card by 10 and adding 40. This means that the last digit of the answer is unaffected by the number of the card, and so can be used to identify the suit.

The suit only depends on the final digit of the answer, so we'll concentrate on the instructions that deal with the last digit. When the instructions say "add 20 for a red card and 21 for a black card", then the last digit will be 0 for red or 1 for black. Next you multiply by 2, therefore the last digit will be 0 for a red diamond or heart and 2 for a black club or spade.

Next, it says to add 1 for a spade or a heart. So looking at the last digits, a red diamond will stay as 0, but a red heart will become 1. A black club will stay as 2 but a black spade will become 3.

A spooky prediction!

Here's a neat think-of-a-number trick you can do with this book.

- Tell Mavis the Phantom X has run off to hide somewhere in this book.

- Mavis has to think of a number *between 1 and 9*. (Or you could pass her a die and ask her to throw it and not tell you which number she gets.)
- Multiply by 2.
- Add 119.
- Multiply by 5.
- The answer should have three digits – Mavis has to CROSS OUT the middle digit to leave a two-digit number.
- Tell Mavis to look for that page number in this book, then look at the bottom of the page.
- Calm her terror by explaining that you only intend to use your awesome magic powers for good and not evil.

You can try this trick on yourself. Think of a number between 1 and 9, follow the instructions and turn to the page!

The reason this works is that if your number is y, the instructions always produce the answer $(10y + 595)$. As long as y is between 1 and 9, the answer will always have a 6 at the front and a 5 at the end. The value of y only affects the middle digit so when you cross that out, you always get the answer 65. Oooh – clever!

The red-and-black miracle

The oil lamps had burnt low around the walls of the Last Chance Saloon as the doors swung open. A man in a long black coat stepped in from the long black night.

"Well, hello Brett!" called Riverboat Lil from the table beside the silent piano.

"Well, goodbye Lil," replied Brett Shuffler immediately turning round to step outside again.

"Where you goin', Brett?"

"I'm going anyplace where I can be sure of leaving with my boots on." But Brett had hesitated for just that moment too long.

"It's gotten mighty late, Brett!" yawned Lil. "And there ain't anyplace else left open. Don't you know what the time is?"

"You know darn well I don't know!" cursed Brett. "The last time we met, you cheated me out of the gold watch and chain that my grandpappy left to me."

"Cheat nothing!" Lil produced the heavy watch from her purse. "You were just unlucky, and I feel sore about that. And every time I look at this time piece, do you know what time it tells me? It tells me it's time you won it back ... so come on over and park your pants, Brett."

Brett turned to watch Lil shuffling an old deck and suddenly felt excited. In Lil's hands, those cards would usually fly back and forth like frogs on a log, but tonight was different. Maybe the hour had gotten too late but Lil was fumbling and dropping them all over the place. Catching Brett's glance, she smiled awkwardly and stooped to pick the jack of clubs off the floor. But as she did so, she accidentally let slip a handful of others. Brett licked his lips. Could this be his big chance? Lil could barely hold on to the pack, let alone deal him a dodgy hand.

"What's the game?" asked Brett as he pulled a chair up to the table. "I've a fancy I could be lucky tonight."

"I'm tired," said Lil. "So how's about something simple? We split the deck, you take all the black cards and I take all the red cards."

"There's a few on the floor," said Brett.

"Who cares?" said Lil. "It's late. Just as long as all my cards are red, and all yours are black. And you do all the dealing Brett. My hands just ain't functioning right tonight."

Brett dealt the cards face up on to the table, giving Lil all the reds and keeping the blacks for himself.

When he'd finished, Lil asked him to turn the two piles of cards face down. Lil spread hers out roughly across the table, while Brett picked his up and held them close. He wasn't taking any chances.

"Now you pass some of your black cards over to me," said Lil.

"How many?" said Brett.

"Many as you like," said Lil. "Pick a number."

"Here's ten," said Brett passing ten cards over face down. Lil mixed them into her pile on the table.

"Now you take ten cards back off the table," she said. "And you shuffle them into your deck."

"I guess I've picked up some red and some black," said Brett shuffling the new cards with the ones he was already holding.

"Guess you have," said Lil. "Now, you pick another number of cards to give me and pass them over. And always keep them face down."

"I'll give you eight this time," said Brett. "Guess there's a real mixture of red and black now."

"Guess there is," said Lil, mixing Brett's eight cards in with the others on the table. "OK, Brett, now you pick any eight cards and put them back in your hand. Then look at all the cards you're holding. And don't show me."

So Brett picked eight cards, put them with his others then opened them out to inspect them.

"Good mixture of red and black, Brett?" asked Lil.

"Pretty good," said Brett.

"You started with all black cards?" said Lil. "But now you got some of my red ones too, right?"

"Right," said Brett. "And I guess you've got some of my black ones."

"I daresay," said Lil, "although I ain't looked yet. But I'll wager this nice gold watch against your boots that I finished up with more of your black cards than you got of my red cards."

Brett stared at his hand and counted seven red cards. He desperately wanted that watch back – but did Lil have more than seven black cards? He knew that a normal pack has 26 red and 26 black cards so he should be able to work it out but...

Brett thought hard. It seemed like a fair game and after all, Lil had hardly touched the cards, but still he was suspicious.

"I've got it!" he exclaimed. "If you want to bet you've got more of my black cards, then you must know something, Lil! I say we turn this around. How about you wager that I got more of your red cards?"

"Whatever you say, Brett," said Lil. "Because I don't really want your boots and I sure would like to give you this watch back."

But Brett still wasn't happy. Could he be sure that Lil had more than seven black cards? Lil *never* lost a bet, even for a pair of boots. With a sigh he rose to leave.

"Now where you goin'?" asked Lil sweetly.

"You're bluffin' me somehow," said Brett. "And you're making me bet when I don't want to, so I'm leaving."

"Brett!" wailed Lil. "Sit down. Look, I'll make it as easy as I can. I'll let you win both ways. If you got more of my red cards, you win. OR ... if I got more of your black cards, you win again. It's either gonna be you or it's gonna be you. What do you say?"

"So whoever got more of the other person's cards, I win?" Brett hurriedly checked the seven red cards in his hand. None of them had turned black or blue or any other colour. "You got a bet, lady!"

Then, one by one, Lil turned over the cards on the table. Brett's eyes nearly fell out of his head as the seventh and last black card turned up.

"Mighty me!" said Lil. "I just don't believe your luck, Brett. I've got the same number of your black cards as you've got of my red cards. So nobody got more and so I guess you don't win."

The mechanics of this trick are extremely simple! It doesn't matter how many cards are on the floor, or what colour they are. Furthermore, it doesn't matter how many cards Brett passes over and takes back, it doesn't even matter how many times he does it. The only important thing is that *Brett must end up holding exactly the same number of cards as he starts with!*

Let C =   the number of cards Brett starts and ends with.

Let b =   the number of black cards that Brett has ended up giving to Lil by the time the game finishes. (So black cards that he's passed over and then taken back don't count.)

Let r =   the number of red cards that Brett has finished up holding at the end of the game.

Here's what happens:
● At the start of the game, all the cards Brett is holding are black. So he starts with C black cards.

- By the end of the game Brett has passed over b black cards, so the number of black cards he's still got is $C - b$.
- Also, by the end of the game Brett has taken r red cards from Lil. So the total numbers of black and red cards he is holding at the end is $C - b + r$.
- But at the end of the game we know that he is holding C cards, therefore: $C - b + r = C$.
- If you re-arrange the equation you get $C - C + r = b$, but of course $C - C = 0$, so then you're just left with $r = b$.

This tells us that he gets as many red cards from Lil as he gives black cards to her. The two numbers *have* to be the same!

THE MURDEROUS MATHS TESTING LABORATORY

So far in this book, we've found out how algebra can solve problems and do tricks for us, but now it's time to meet some of the experts who really push it to the limits. As a special treat, we're going to sneak you into the Murderous Maths testing laboratory where the Pure Mathematicians pin down ugly expressions and equations and do ghastly experiments on them.

Before you go in, you've got to look the part. Get rid of any groovy clothes such as baseball caps, trainers or jeans. You'll need to wear any or all of the following: an orange nylon shirt or blouse, a tie or brooch with a wacky cartoon character on it, a greeny-grey cardigan with holes where the buttons used to be, trousers that don't quite reach down to the top of your socks, a belt that doesn't actually go through any of the belt loops on your trousers, wrinkled tights, a faded badge saying "National Maths Conference Delegate July 1983" and if you can't create your own natural dandruff then sprinkle some breadcrumbs on your shoulders. Above all, you need a BIG SMILE, because you are permanently happy to be living in a world that is full of lovely sums. Oh, and one more thing – be sure to carry a half-empty plastic cup of cold coffee with you. It mustn't be a full cup and it mustn't be a warm cup, because for some mysterious reason that just wouldn't be right.

Ready? (Whoops – don't forget to check your shirt tail is hanging out.) In we go then...

Immediately, your eye is drawn to the dissection bench in the middle of the room. What is that ugly expression the Mathematicians have got pinned down on it?

Eh? How can they say it's nothing? It's a horrible mess of letters and brackets. Obviously they are having some sort of mathematical private joke. Bless 'em. Let's print it up and have another look and see if we can see what's so amusing:

$$\frac{(b+a)(2b-a)(a-b)^2}{(b-a)(b^2-a^2)(2b-a)} - 1$$

It's unbelievable, but they are even madder than usual today. Can you see what's so funny? Is it the big dividing line, or maybe the "squares" dotted about the place. It would help if we knew what a or b were. Maybe the letter "a" represents some hilarious comedy item?

93

If they're going to be silly, we'll just ignore them. Come on, let's have a look round and see what's pinned on the notice board.

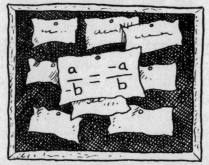

That's handy! If you have a minus sign on the bottom of a fraction, you can just move it to the top. This is because you can always multiply the top and bottom of a fraction by the same number without upsetting anything. In this case you just multiply through by −1. You get:

$$\frac{a}{-b} = \frac{a \times -1}{-b \times -1} = \frac{-a}{b}$$

Simple but satisfying.

That's very kind. You pass over your half-empty plastic cup of cold coffee and look round. What else is there?

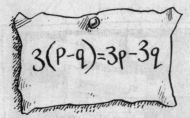

$$3(p-q)=3p-3q$$

We knew that. Brackets are a way of saying everything inside has to be multiplied by the coefficient outside.

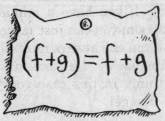

$$(f+g)=f+g$$

Same thing. If a bracket hasn't got a number outside, then the coefficient is just +1. So you can just take the brackets away if you like.

Oh boy! You'll never guess what's bothering them. Even if you're happy that $(f + g) = f + g$ there are some Pure Mathematicians that say you can't turn it round and put $f + g = (f + g)$

This is one of those times when you just want to scream, isn't it? Never mind, at least one of them has a bit of common sense…

Phew. So let's all agree that $(f + g) = f + g$ AND $f + g = (f + g)$ and if anyone disagrees with you, go and make them two omelettes. That should settle the matter and if they still want to argue, don't worry. Nobody takes anybody seriously if they are spitting out bits of egg while they're talking.

❌ If you change the sign outside a bracket, change the signs inside too.

This is a useful little trick. The reason it works is that $-(r-s)$ has a coefficient of -1 outside the bracket. We don't bother putting in the "1" because it doesn't make any difference, but the minus makes a LOT of difference. When you expand $-(r-s)$ here's what happens to the two letters: $-1 \times r = -r$ and $-1 \times -s = +s$. When you put these results together you get $-r + s$. We can swap them round to give $s - r$ and then, as the omelettes showed us, $s - r = (s - r)$.

There's just one more thing pinned on the notice board:

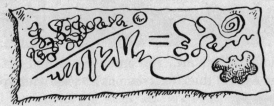

Wow! This looks complicated. Presumably it's some sort of higher dimensional algebra used in the analysis of compound infinities?

ER... NOT QUITE. I WAS JUST TESTING MY BIRO WAS WORKING...

AND THAT'S WHERE I KEEP MY CHEWING GUM!

Something strangely satisfying

So much for the notice board, now let's see what's on the shelf.

PASCAL'S COEFFICIENTS

What's this about? The only way to find out is to expand each of these expressions and see what we get.

$(a - b) = a - b$
That's easy enough.

$(a - b)^2$ is a little bit tougher. It means $(a - b)(a - b)$ and to work it out you have to multiply everything in the first bracket by everything in the second bracket. If you're not sure what you're doing, the safest way is to split the first bracket into the two terms a and $-b$, then multiply each term by the second bracket. You get this:

$$(a - b)(a - b) = a(a - b) - b(a - b) = a^2 - ab - ba + b^2$$

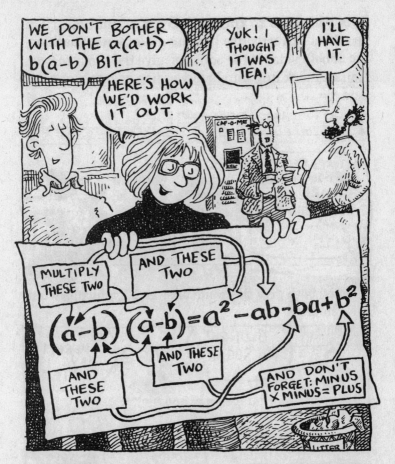

Once you've got $a^2 - ab - ba + b^2$ you look for "like terms" which you might remember are terms with the same combinations of letters. Here we've got $-ab$ and $-ba$ which both have one a and one b. (It doesn't matter which way round they are.) So we can put them together and get $-2ab$. The final answer is:

$$(a - b)^2 = a^2 - 2ab + b^2$$

If you want to check that you've multiplied out brackets correctly, try putting in some numbers and see if both sides of the equation give the same answer. You can pick any numbers you like so let's say $a = 7$ and $b = 3$.

- $(a - b)^2 = (7 - 3)^2 = 4^2 = 16$
- $a^2 - 2ab + b^2 = 7^2 - 2 \times 7 \times 3 + 3^2 = 49 - 42 + 9 = 16$

ALWAYS REMEMBER TO MULTIPLY BEFORE YOU DO THE + AND - BITS.

They both give the same answer 16, which is what we'd hoped.

BLURGH! NO SUGAR!

LEAVE IT THERE. I'LL HAVE IT LATER.

SPLONK

While we're at it, what do you think $(a + b)^2$ makes? (We've swapped the minus for a plus in the bracket in case you didn't spot it.) If you multiply it out you get exactly the same answer, only there aren't any minus signs!

$$(a + b)^2 = a^2 + 2ab + b^2$$

Let's do a quick test again with $a = 7$ and $b = 3$:

- $(a + b)^2 = (7 + 3)^2 = 10^2 = 100$
- $a^2 + 2ab + b^2 = 7^2 + 2 \times 7 \times 3 + 3^2 = 49 + 42 + 9 = 100$

The little "something-and-a-half squared" trick

$(a + b)^2$ leads to a rather nifty short cut if you want to work out "something-and-a-half" squared. You multiply the "something" by the next number up and add a quarter.

So if you need to work out $(5\frac{1}{2})^2$ you multiply 5×6 to get 30, then you add $\frac{1}{4}$. You get $(5\frac{1}{2})^2 = 30\frac{1}{4}$.

You can see this always works if you multiply out $(a + \frac{1}{2})^2$. You get: $(a + \frac{1}{2})(a + \frac{1}{2}) = a^2 + 2 \times a \times \frac{1}{2} + \frac{1}{2} \times \frac{1}{2} = a^2 + a + \frac{1}{4} = a(a + 1) + \frac{1}{4}$

Suppose you've got a square floor that you want to cover with square tiles. You can get $8\frac{1}{2}$ tiles along one edge. How many tiles do you need in total? You need to work out $(8\frac{1}{2})^2$ so the "a" in the equation becomes 8.

You get $(8 + \frac{1}{2})^2 = 8(8 + 1) + \frac{1}{4} = 8 \times 9 + \frac{1}{4} = 72\frac{1}{4}$

Now let's see what happens when we expand this beauty.

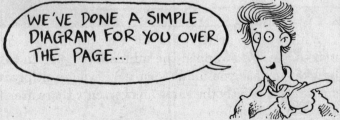

WE'VE DONE A SIMPLE DIAGRAM FOR YOU OVER THE PAGE...

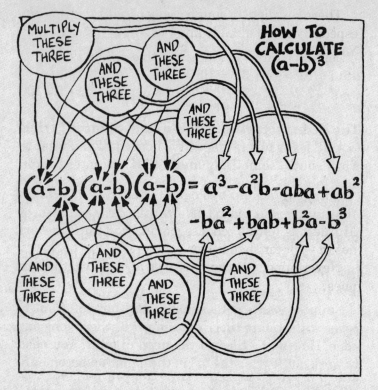

Now we bring the like terms together, and the trick is to spot them all! For instance: $aba = ba^2 = a^2b$ and also $ab^2 = bab = b^2a$. We finish with:

$$(a - b)^3 = a^3 - 3a^2b + 3ab^2 - b^3$$

There's a slightly simpler way of working this out, especially as we already know $(a - b)^2 = (a^2 - 2ab + b^2)$ You do this:

$$
\begin{aligned}
(a - b)^3 &= (a - b)(a - b)^2 \\
&= (a - b)(a^2 - 2ab + b^2) \\
&= a(a^2 - 2ab + b^2) - b(a^2 - 2ab + b^2) \\
&= a^3 - 2a^2b + ab^2 - ba^2 + 2ab^2 - b^3 \\
&= a^3 - 3a^2b + 3ab^2 - b^3
\end{aligned}
$$

Sorry, we should apologize. This book has ruined the fun for you, hasn't it? We'd forgotten that keen Murderous Maths readers would have liked to work out $(a - b)^3$ for themselves.

Never mind, you can have a go at checking the next ones...

$$(a - b)^4 = a^4 - 4a^3b + 6a^2b^2 - 4ab^3 + b^4$$

Does that look right to you? Good. Now check this one:

$$(a - b)^5 = a^5 - 5a^4b + 10a^3b^2 - 10a^2b^3 + 5ab^4 - b^5$$

By now you might have spotted a few patterns in the answers. As you look along the terms you'll see:
● The signs go − + − + alternately.
● The powers of "a" reduce one at a time.
● The powers of "b" increase one at a time.

So if we wanted to work out $(a - b)^6$ we could be fairly sure it looks like this:

$$a^6 - \square a^5b + \square a^4b^2 - \square a^3b^3 + \square a^2b^4 - \square ab^5 + b^6$$

The only bits we don't know are the coefficients to put in the boxes. Wouldn't it be great if we didn't have to do TONNES of multiplying out to find the answer? Stand by for some amazing news...

If you've read *Do You Feel Lucky?* you'll already know about Pascal's Triangle and some of the amazing things it does. You're about to discover one more, but first let's see what it looks like:

As you can see, the triangle has a row of ones down each side. Each number inside the triangle is made by adding the two numbers above it. So on the second row, the 2 comes from 1 + 1. On the next row each of the 3s comes from 1 + 2. Further down the number 21 comes from 6 + 15 and so on. You can write out as many rows as you like, but we've just put seven here.

HELP!

URGH! WHAT'S THIS FLY DOING IN HERE?

SWIMMING! Ho Ho!

Now let's look at the coefficients we got for our powers of $(a - b)$:

THE SUM   **THE COEFFICIENTS** (WITHOUT +/- SIGNS)

$(a-b) = a - b$ 1 1

$(a-b)^2 = a^2 - 2ab + b^2$ 1 2 1

$(a-b)^3 = a^3 - 3a^2b + 3ab^2 - b^3$ 1 3 3 1

$(a-b)^4 = a^4 - 4a^3b + 6a^2b^2 - 4ab^3 + b^4$ 1 4 6 4 1

$(a-b)^5 = a^5 - 5a^4b + 10a^3b^2 - 10a^2b^3 + 5ab^4 - b^5$ 1 5 10 10 5 1

Amazingly enough, the coefficients are exactly the same as the numbers on each line of Pascal's Triangle! So for $(a - b)^6$ we just use the numbers from the sixth line of the triangle:

$$(a - b)^6 = a^6 - 6a^5b + 15a^4b^2 - 20a^3b^3 + 15a^2b^4 - 6ab^5 + b^6$$

And even...

$$(a - b)^7 = a^7 - 7a^6b + 21a^5b^2 - 35a^4b^3 + 35a^3b^4 - 21a^2b^5 + 7ab^6 - b^7$$

But if you want to check $(a - b)^7$, do help yourself. Here's what you need to work out:

$(a - b)(a - b)(a - b)(a - b)(a - b)(a - b)(a - b) = \ldots?$

NOW LOOK AT THIS!

The DIFFERENCE BETWEEN TWO SQUARES

GOT IT!

BUZZ! COUGH! GASP!

So far we've had $(a - b)^2$ which is $(a - b)(a - b)$. If you look back carefully you'll also see $(a + b)^2$ which is $(a + b)(a + b)$. But one of the cutest tricks in maths is when you take one $(a - b)$ bracket and multiply it with one $(a + b)$ bracket.

$$(a + b)(a - b) = a(a - b) + b(a - b)$$
$$= a^2 - ab + ba - b^2 = a^2 - b^2$$

Yes, the $-ab$ and the $+ba$ cancel each other out! So we get:

✗ $a^2 - b^2 = (a + b)(a - b)$

THIS ONE IS AWESOME, SO DON'T FORGET IT!

CLICK!

This neat little result is so useful that it's marked with the hot-tip sign. And if you don't trust algebra, then read *Numbers: the Key to the Universe*. It tells you how you can prove that this equation always works just using patterns of counters!

Here's how people describe this smashing equation in words set to four-part harmony:

THE DIFFERENCE OF TWO SQUARES IS THE SUM TIMES THE DIFFERENCE... DOO SHOOBY DOOBY DOO WAH!

Here's what it means:
- "The difference of two squares" is when you take one squared number from another, so that's the same as saying $a^2 - b^2$.
- The "sum" is when you add the two numbers together, which is $(a + b)$.
- The "difference" is when you take one number from the other, which is $(a - b)$.
- If you multiply the sum and difference together you get $(a + b)(a - b)$.

WHO WAS THIS COFFEE FOR ANYWAY?

DUNNO

Here's just one trick you can use this for:

Suppose you want to know what 98^2 is, but you really can't be bothered to work out 98×98? You can use the simple fact that $100^2 = 10,000$ and obviously 98^2 is a bit smaller. So how much do you need to take away from 100^2 to get 98^2?

You need to know "the difference of two squares", which is the sum $(100 + 98)$ multiplied by the difference $(100 - 98)$. This comes out as $198 \times 2 = 396$.

All you do now to work out 98^2 is $10,000 - 396$, which equals $9,604$. That's the answer!

How about 203^2? 200^2 is simple enough, it's $40,000$. Obviously 203^2 is a bit bigger, and the difference is $(203 + 200)(203 - 200) = 403 \times 3 = 1,209$. Therefore $203^2 = 40,000 + 1,209 = 41,209$.

Time to leave

So that's about it, then. We've seen all the strange bits on display and we can't wait any longer for that cup of coffee we were offered, so it's time to head for the door. The only thing we haven't found out is why the Pure Mathematicians are laughing at this:

$$\frac{(b + a)(2b - a)(a - b)^2}{(b - a)(b^2 - a^2)(2b - a)} - 1$$

And yes, they are STILL laughing. What's so funny?

That does it. Before we go, let's mess it around and see if we can find out what this big joke is for ourselves.

No we are NOT! We've already seen what happens when we have to multiply lots of brackets together. In fact, here's another tip:

❌ Don't multiply brackets out until you have to. (Or unless you really want to, of course. Some people enjoy it.)

Quite often, you can get rid of brackets before you do any fancy sums, so let's see if anything will just cancel and disappear ... and what do we find? There's a $(2b - a)$ bracket on the top AND another one on the bottom, so we're going to cancel them out! Well why not?

If you had $\frac{15f}{5}$, you could just divide the top and bottom by 5 and get $\frac{3f}{1}$ which is the same as $3f$. If you had $\frac{a}{8ab}$ that would become $\frac{1}{8b}$. With brackets it isn't any harder, just look out for brackets that are exactly the same.

$$\frac{(c + 2d)}{(c + 2d)} = 1 \quad \text{or} \quad \frac{7(m - p)}{8(m - p)} = \frac{7}{8}$$

$$\text{or} \quad \frac{(r - s)(r + s)}{(r + s)(r - 2s)} = \frac{(r - s)}{(r - 2s)}$$

You'll see with the last example, you can cancel out the $(r + s)$ on the top and bottom, but you can't do much with the $(r - s)$ and $(r - 2s)$ because they are different.

111

$$\frac{(b+a)(a-b)^2}{(b-a)(b^2-a^2)} - 1$$

It looks a little bit nicer, but it's still not exactly funny, so now what? The brackets are all different, but what happens if we give the $(b^2 - a^2)$ a prod? As it's the difference of two squares it will turn into $(b+a)(b-a)$. Let's put it in then:

$$\frac{(b+a)(a-b)^2}{(b-a)(b+a)(b-a)} - 1$$

That gives us $(b+a)$ on the top and the bottom! They cancel out too:

$$\frac{(a-b)^2}{(b-a)(b-a)} - 1$$

This is looking better! How are we doing?

Wouldn't it be great if we could turn the two $(b-a)$ brackets round so that they both become $(a-b)$?

GO ON THEN! JUST REMEMBER TO CHANGE THE SIGN OUTSIDE!

She's right! Look at the bottom line. If we start with $(b-a)(b-a)$ we can turn the first bracket round and add a minus sign to make it into $-(a-b)(b-a)$. Let's try it, and while we're at it we'll make the $(a-b)^2$ on the top line into $(a-b)(a-b)$.

$$\frac{(a-b)(a-b)}{-(a-b)(b-a)} - 1$$

We can cancel an $(a-b)$ from top and bottom! Great.

$$\frac{(a-b)}{-(b-a)} - 1$$

Just a minute, look what's on the bottom! $-(b-a)$ is the same as $(a-b)$.

$$\frac{(a-b)}{(a-b)} - 1$$

and then the whole thing cancels to make: $1-1$

NOW DO YOU SEE THE JOKE? YOU ASKED WHAT'S SO FUNNY... AND WE SAID "NOTHING"! AND OF COURSE 1-1=0!

And so, as another merry day comes to a close in the Murderous Maths testing laboratory, it's time for us to sneak away. If you didn't quite follow all the algebra, at least there's another mystery to think about: how come you're still holding a half-empty plastic cup of cold coffee? As you can see, it takes a very special kind of person to be a Pure Mathematician but you have to admit, they're happy. If everybody on the planet were like them, then maybe the world would be a better place. Who knows?

THE BANK CLOCK

City: **Chicago, Illinois, USA**
Place: **The Municipal Park**
Date: **5 October 1928**
Time: **6.32 pm (and 44 seconds)**

As the sun gave up for the day and collapsed towards the horizon, the Theobald Butcher memorial fountain suddenly belched and died. Every one of the 27 giant jets had choked to a stop, leaving just a few lonely drips to break the silence.

"Wow!" came a hushed chorus of deep voices. "It really happens!"

A bewildered pigeon perched on Theobald's stone tuba looked around to see where the whispering had come from. The park seemed completely deserted, save for the bench in the nearby bushes where an enormous newspaper was being held open. From underneath the bottom edge of the paper protruded fourteen trousered legs.

"So tell us, Blade," came the Weasel's voice from behind the paper. "How is the fountain stopping gonna help us rob the City Bank?"

115

"Yeah," said Chainsaw Charlie. "How come we don't need guns? You just said to bring bags and torches."

"Shut the talk!" hissed Blade Boccelli, lowering his end of the newspaper and looking around nervously. He spotted the pigeon that had fluttered down to see if the men had dropped anything edible under the bench. "Hey you, birdie. Shoo!"

The pigeon looked up and was amazed to find itself staring into the barrel of Half-smile Gabrianni's revolver.

"He means it," drawled Half-smile. "Go make a nest or lay eggs or something. This is a private business meeting."

Without bothering to rush, the pigeon made her way back up to Theobald's tuba. It was a disappointing start to her evening.

"Well, Blade?" said the Weasel, lowering the other end of the paper. "We still wanna know about the bank."

"It's like this..." said Blade. "The fountain is on the same electric circuit as the bank."

"And so when the fountain goes off, the power in the bank goes off, too?"

"That's it," said Blade. "And when the power goes off, it takes exactly two minutes to reset itself and come back on again. Numbers is checking the time right now."

"It's been off for 23 seconds so far," said the thin man with the big watch.

"That's awesome!" gasped Chainsaw. "You mean, the bank ain't got no juice for two minutes?"

"That's just beautiful," chuckled Jimmy. "Imagine two

116

whole minutes of a bank without an alarm system..."

"It gets better," said Blade. "If the power shuts off at night, there's no lights either, so that's two minutes when seven smart guys with torches and bags can dash around scooping up the sweet green stuff! While they're all panicking, we'll be packing. What do you say, fellas?"

"You're a genius, Blade!" said Porky Boccelli.

"Why, thank you, little brother," said Blade, who was trying not to blush as all the others nodded in agreement. "But this has got to be our secret, right? You all gotta swear not to tell a living soul."

"We all swear not to tell a living soul that you're a genius," they solemnly promised.

"Why does the power short out?" asked Chainsaw.

"It's to do with the City Bank clock," said Blade.

"And how does the clock short the power out?" persisted Chainsaw.

"Don't go forcing me into the technicalities," said Blade. "You guys' brains couldn't handle that level of information."

"Try us," said the six other men.

"Er..." struggled Blade, "the clock's got a long hand and a short hand, right? Well the short hand shorts out the power. That's why it's called the short hand. Obviously."

"But I still don't see..."

"Shaddup! Someone's coming!" snapped Blade, hurriedly pulling the newspaper back up in front of their faces.

Sure enough, a pair of elegant heels was clicking down the path towards them. A secretary taking an evening stroll? Maybe she had a muffin with a few loose crumbs to spare. The pigeon hopped down and strutted towards the heels hopefully.

"Scram!" snapped a cold voice. "Or I'll stitch your beak, you ragged little buzzard."

The pigeon hadn't survived three years in this park without knowing when to scram, so, very wisely, she scrammed. This was not turning into a good evening for pigeons. The heels approached the newspaper and stopped.

"Hello, Blade."

"You got the wrong person, ma'am," came the reply from behind the paper.

"And you got last Tuesday's paper, Blade."

Slowly, the newspaper was lowered and the seven men looked sheepishly towards the lady in the heels and the tight pink coat.

"What you doing, Blade?" snapped Dolly Snowlips. "I told you to keep these geeks out of sight until sundown."

"We were just checking Blade's plan was going to work," said Chainsaw.

"Whose plan?" Dolly was unimpressed. "Since when did Blade ever have a plan?"

"Hey!" said Blade. "It was me that thought of taking bags in with us to hold the money. Dolly just supplied all the other details."

"So how do we know when the next power cut's gonna be, then, Dolly?" asked Weasel.

"Why don't you ask Blade?" sneered Dolly. "It's his plan."

"Next time the fountain stops," said Blade.

"Which is when?"

"Er, it's er..." But Blade knew when he was beaten.

"There are two power cables in the clock tower," explained Dolly. "An acquaintance of mine has arranged it so that one cable is fixed to the hour hand and the other cable is fixed to the minute hand of the clock. At the exact moment the minute hand crosses over the hour hand, the two cables touch. And so the power gets shorted out."

All seven men looked up at the clock. Sure enough, the fountain had stopped just as the minute hand passed over the hour hand.

"So as soon as the hands cross, you got two minutes before the power breaker resets itself," said Dolly. "The time is now approaching 6:35. The next time the hands cross, it'll be dark, so I suggest you get over to the bank and be ready. You don't want to waste a single second of cash-and-carry time, do you now?"

"No, ma'am," they chorused.

"Then I'll see you all later at Luigi's for the split," said Dolly as she turned and set off. Without looking back, she called, "And don't mess this one up."

"That's the two minutes done!" announced Numbers, checking his watch. "The power should be back on."

"So why ain't the fountain squirting water again?" demanded Weasel.

"Hey, listen!" said Chainsaw, who had gone over to inspect it. "I can hear the pump pumping. If you put your ear to a squirty hole, you can hear the water coming back up the pipes!"

Half-smile Gabrianni also put his ear to the fountain.

"It sounds like Porky's gut after a nine-course dinner!" laughed Half-smile. "Come here, guys. You gotta hear this."

The pigeon looked down from Theobald's tuba in disbelief as all the men rushed to put their ears to the squirty holes in the fountain. And when the water suddenly shot out, she felt it hadn't been such a bad evening after all.

Place: Outside the City Bank
Time: 7.00 pm

The seven men were all leaning casually against the same lamppost, pretending to read the same paper. A pool of water had formed under their feet and was slowly spreading across the sidewalk.

"It's getting kind of dark, Blade," said Porky.

"That's because the sun's gone down," said Blade.

"Just like I planned it."

"How much time have we got to wait?" said Half-smile. "I wanna go home and get into some dry clothes. This fountain water stinks and it's freezing."

"We wait until the big hand crosses the little hand," said Blade.

"So how long will that be?" said Half-smile.

"It's seven o'clock now," said Blade. "So the short hand is on the seven and the hour hand is on the twelve. The question is, how long will it take the hour hand to move round to the seven?"

"Thirty-five minutes," said Numbers.

"We g-got to wait thirty-five m-minutes?" shivered Chainsaw. "I'm getting c-chilly in these wet pants."

"M-me too," said One-Finger Jimmy. "I don't wanna catch the influenza or frostbite or icicles or n-nothing."

"C'mon!" said Blade. "Soon you'll be so rich, you'll be lighting fires with fifties. Ain't that worth waiting thirty-five minutes for?"

"Guess so," they all muttered.

Place: Still outside the City Bank
Time: 7.30 pm
Under the glare of the street lamp, the newspaper was starting to quiver.

"Hold it steady, can't ya?" said Porky. "I'm trying to read today's recipe."

"I can't h-help it," shivered the Weasel. "I'm s-shaking my s-socks off. H-how much l-longer we got to wait for the power to shut off?"

"The time's now seven-thirty," said Blade. "So just five more minutes and the big hand will reach the seven and cross the little hand."

121

"But … but look!" gasped Chainsaw. "The little hand, it ain't on the seven no more. It's moved on!"

The newspaper fell to the ground.

"Never thought of that, d-did you, Blade?" muttered Half-smile through his chattering teeth. "While the big hand moves, the little hand moves a b-b-bit too!"

"S-so?" said Blade, folding his arms tight and stamping his feet. "We have to wait a couple more minutes for the big hand to catch up."

"Exactly h-how many more m-minutes?" pleaded the Weasel.

"I got it!" said Numbers. "It takes one hour for the little hand to move from the seven to the eight, right?"

"Right," they agreed.

"The time is now half-past seven," said Numbers. "So, the little hand is exactly halfway between the seven and the eight. So, the big hand has to move to halfway between the seven and the eight too. That should take an extra two-and-a-half minutes. In total, that makes it seven-and-a-half minutes from now. "

"I d-don't think I can m-make it!" said Chainsaw.

"M-me neither!" said Jimmy.

"C-come on, guys!" said Blade, trying to sound hot. "What's seven-and-a-half minutes when there's a fortune waiting at the end of it?"

"It's longer than that," said Numbers.

"WHAT?" they all gasped.

"When the big hand has moved round another seven-and-a-half minutes, the little hand will have moved on a teeny little bit more. And when the big hand moves on that same teeny little bit more, the little hand will have moved on just a teeny-weeny little bit more. And when the big hand has moved that teeny-weeny little extra bit, the little hand will have moved just a teeny-weeny-peeny little bit more..."

"So whenever the big hand reaches where the little hand was, the little hand has already moved on!" cried Weasel. "The way I see it, the big hand will *never* catch the little hand!"

"Oh no!" they all chorused.

"That can't be right!" said Blade, but too late. The others were already squelching off as briskly as they could towards the comforting lights and smells of Upper Main Street. Blade was left staring up at the clock.

"So when the big hand gets to where the little hand was, the little hand has already moved on," he muttered. "Boy, you've got to hand it to these banks, they sure know how to design a clever clock."

Thrusting his hands deep into his pockets he hurried after the gang.

Place: Luigi's Diner, Upper Main Street
Time: 7.34 pm
"I don't believe this!" snapped Dolly. "Whaddya mean, the hands will never cross each other?"

The seven men shivering around the table tried again.

"You see, whenever the big hand moves to where the little hand was…"

"The little hand has moved on a bit more…"

"And so the big hand has to move a little bit more…"

"And while it does the little hand moves another little bit more…"

"Give me strength!" shouted Dolly.

Luigi rushed over from behind his counter.

"Sorry, Miss Snowlips," he apologized. "I had no idea you were ready to order."

"Well, I am," said Dolly. "I want a big glass of Vino Pronto."

"And for you gentlemen?" asked Luigi.

"S-something hot," shivered Weasel. "As hot as you've got."

"You want hot?" said Luigi. "Oh, boy! Today I can give you hot. We got a big lot of soup, but maybe the soup we got is a lot too hot."

"Whaddya mean, t-too hot?" said Chainsaw.

"It was supposed to be peppered chilli lobster soup," explained Luigi. "Only Benni forgot to get lobsters. So trust me, it's hot."

"Then g-go get it!" said Half-smile. "All of it, and fast!"

Luigi hurried away.

"Look, you numbskulls," explained Dolly. "Imagine a clock says seven o'clock, right?"

"Right."

"And then it says eight o'clock."

"Right."

"How did the big hand get all the way round without crossing the little hand?"

"Er…"

124

"You dupes!" cursed Dolly. "Of course it crosses over."
"OK, so it crosses over," said Blade. "But *when?*"

Let's start with the hands indicating seven o'clock.

As we're dealing with the hands moving around the clock face, the distance that they travel is important. The easiest way to measure the distance is in "minutes", so if a hand travels all the way round the clock face, that's a "distance" of 60 minutes. Obviously, the big hand will move a "distance" of one minute in one minute of time, but for now we'll ignore that.

The question we need to answer is – how many minutes does the big hand have to travel before it crosses the little hand? Let's call it m.

We can divide the distance the big hand travels into two bits.

- First of all, the big hand has to get from the 12 round to the seven. It moves a distance of 35 minutes.

125

- The big hand still has to move a bit more. This bit is the distance that the little hand moves while the big hand moves the total distance of m minutes. We'll call this extra distance e.

If we add up the distances, it's obvious that: $m = 35 + e$.

All we do now is work out e, which is simple enough if you think it through...

In 12 hours, the big hand goes round the clock 12 times and the little hand goes round once. This means that the little hand only moves $\frac{1}{12}$ of the distance of the big hand. So, while the big hand moves a distance of m minutes, the little hand moves a distance of $\frac{m}{12}$ minutes. And so we have $e = \frac{m}{12}$.

Let's go back to Blade's problem. We've got:

$m = 35 + e$ and $e = \frac{m}{12}$ and so:

$m = 35 + \frac{m}{12}$ One unknown! We can solve it.

First multiply everything by 12.

$12m = 420 + m$ Now subtract m from both sides.

$11m = 420$ And then divide through by 11 to get...

$m = \frac{420}{11} = 38 \cdot 182$ minutes

Remember that m is the distance the minute hand moves. When this is measured in time, this will take m minutes. $38 \cdot 182$ minutes is a funny sort of time though, so to be really cool we convert the $0 \cdot 182$ minutes into seconds and get $0 \cdot 182 \times 60 =$ about 11 seconds. We've done it! Let's see the final answer...

THE HANDS ON THE BANK CLOCK WILL CROSS AT 7.38 AND 11 SECONDS.

Luigi put a big glass of Vino Pronto in front of Dolly.

"There you are ma'am," said Luigi. "And Benni's gonna be right here with that soup already."

Dolly raised her glass.

"Here's to nothing," she said, taking a deep slurp. "I can't believe you doiks won't be at the bank when the power goes off."

"I still don't see how or when the two hands cross," said Weasel.

"Yeah," said Chainsaw. "For all we know, this power-cut thing might never happen."

"Of course it's gonna happen!" said Dolly shoving back her chair and marching over to Luigi's wall clock. "Look at the time, it's 7:38. And wouldn't you say the hands are getting pretty close?"

"Soup's up, gentlemen!" called Benni the waiter, as he struggled towards the table with a massive tureen that was shrouded in green steam.

"I tell you," said Dolly, "the power that goes to the bank and the fountain and a whole load of other places is gonna cut out any time now, so don't say I didn't..."

And just as Benni caught his foot on Dolly's chair, the entire restaurant went dark. Seven screams split the air as two gallons of boiling peppered chilli soup cascaded everywhere.

"...warn you."

AXES, PLOTS AND THE FLIGHT OF THE LOVEBURGER

If you fancy an evening out in Brownpool-on-Sea, here's a handy map with five of the main attractions marked on it:

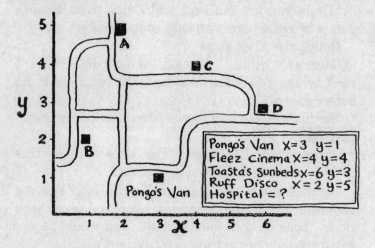

There's a line along the bottom marked "x" and a line up the side marked "y". You'll see that Pongo's van is directly above the number 3 on the x line and straight across from the number 1 on the y line. So to describe Pongo's exact position on the map you just say x = 3 and y = 1.

Can you work out which letters on the map correspond to the cinema, the sunbed salon and the disco? But the most important thing you'll need to know after an evening out at Brownpool is – which letter on the map represents the hospital? How would you describe where the hospital is with x and y?

Answers: cinema C, sunbeds D, disco A, hospital B ($x = 1$ $y = 2$)

When you use two numbers to describe a place on a map, these are called **co-ordinates.** In maths, the x line that goes along the bottom is called the x **axis** and the y line up the side is called the y **axis**. If you put them together you get two **axes**, which once led to a rather unfortunate incident for Urgum the Axeman's maths teacher.

129

To save confusion, these days we pronounce maths axes as "ack-seez" rather than "ack-sez".

❌ Here's a silly way to remember which one's the *x* axis. Imagine that the *y* axis has just knocked *x* axis over, and that the *x* axis is lying on the floor, with the *y* axis still standing up. The one lying on the floor is quite upset, in fact it's a little cross and that's what the *x* is – a little cross.

Nearly everybody knows a bit about using co-ordinates to describe an exact point on a map, but now we're going to chuck away beautiful Brownpool-on-Sea and replace it with a nice clean bit of graph paper.

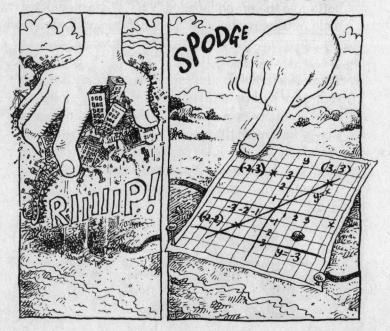

130

Graph paper is marked out in tiny squares to make marking points and measuring lengths easy. Once you've drawn in a pair of axes, you can do tonnes of amazing things. You can make axes any length you like, depending on what numbers you want to use, and here we've even made them cross over so we can have some negative numbers too. There are also a few details to show how it all works:

- There is a little cross at $x = -2$ and $y = 3$. When people describe co-ordinates on a graph they don't usually bother putting in the "$x =$" and "$y =$", they would just say this point is at $(-2,3)$. The secret of this is to remember that the "x" value always comes first, because x comes before y in the alphabet.

- There is a straight line that goes right across the bottom of the graph labelled "$y = -3$". If you made a little mark anywhere on this line, the y co-ordinate would be $y = -3$. Therefore rather cleverly this line is called $y = -3$.

- There is also a diagonal line called $y = x$. This might sound tricky, but it's dead simple! This line joins up *every* point on the graph where the x co-ordinate and y co-ordinate are the same. If you mark a little cross anywhere on the line, you'll find that $y = x$. The points $(3,3)$ and $(-2,-2)$ are marked to show you.

- There is a discarded burger at $(3,-2)$.

STRANGE...

...IT'S TURKEY-AND-MARMALADE FLAVOUR!

How to draw pictures of equations

One of the strangest things in maths is that if you have an equation with two unknowns, you can turn it into a line on a graph. The simplest equation that you can have with two unknowns is $y = x$ and we've just seen the line it makes on the last diagram. Now we'll see how some fancier equations look. These equations almost always start with "$y =$" and then there's some more complicated stuff on the x side.

Let's see how to draw: $y = 2x - 3$

The trick is to work out a few values of x and y that fit the equation, then mark these on the graph. This is called **plotting** some **points**. When you've done this, you join them all up with a line.

- First, pick a value for x, then work out what y should be by putting your x value into the equation. You can choose x to be anything you like. To make things simple go for $x = 0$. When this is put in the equation, you get $y = 2 \times 0 - 3 = -3$. So, if $x = 0$ then $y = -3$.

- Now you can plot the point $(0, -3)$ on the graph with a tiny little cross.

- Go through a few more values for x and see what you get for y. The slickest way to do it is to draw a table.

Ho ho ho. Sorry, we couldn't resist that joke. The trouble is that it will now take several minutes for our murderous artist to stop laughing, wipe his eyes and settle down again. Are you ready, Mr Reeve?

Yes, just about, snigger snigger...

As we were saying, here's a table for $y = 2x - 3$ and we've used values of x from –2 to +3. This gives us a row of points to mark on the graph.

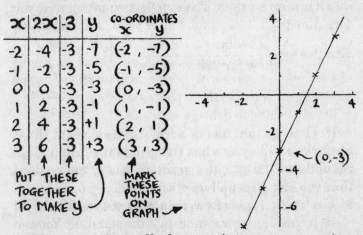

x	2x	-3	y	CO-ORDINATES x y
-2	-4	-3	-7	(-2 , -7)
-1	-2	-3	-5	(-1 , -5)
0	0	-3	-3	(0 , -3)
1	2	-3	-1	(1 , -1)
2	4	-3	+1	(2 , 1)
3	6	-3	+3	(3 , 3)

PUT THESE TOGETHER TO MAKE y

MARK THESE POINTS ON GRAPH ➼

When you join all these points up, you get a straight line, and that line represents $y = 2x - 3$. The good bit is that you can pick *any* place on the line and you'll find that $y = 2x - 3$. For instance, look where the line crosses the x axis. You can see the co-ordinates are $(1\frac{1}{2}, 0)$ Therefore, $x = 1\frac{1}{2}$ and $y = 0$ should work with $y = 2x - 3$, and if you try it, it does.

Now, we'll take this equation apart and see how the two different bits affect the graph...

$y = 2x - 3$

Gradient = +2   "y intercept" = -3

- the **gradient** is how steep the line is.
- the *y* **intercept** is where the line crosses over the *y* axis (or the value of *y* when $x = 0$).

Gradients

$$\text{Gradient} = \frac{\text{how far you go up}}{\text{how far you go along}}$$

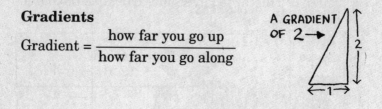

If your graph has a straight line then the *x* coefficient tells you what the gradient of the line is. So with $y = 2x - 3$, the gradient is +2. This means that the line goes up two places for every one place it moves along. Here are some different gradients:

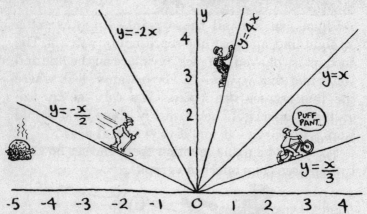

- The steepest line here is $y = 4x$ because "4" is the biggest number.
- $y = \frac{x}{3}$ is the smallest gradient, which is just $\frac{1}{3}$. It might not look much here, but this is about the steepest hill you'll find on any road. If you were on your bike, you'd need to get off and push.

- You'll also see that two of the lines go "downhill" rather than "uphill" and that these gradients have minus signs.
- There is a discarded liver-and-artichoke-flavoured burger at (−5,1).

y intercept

If you look at the lines on this graph, you'll see that each one is marked with the equation that makes it.

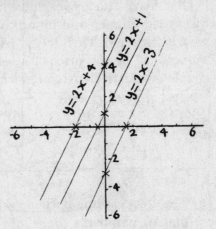

Do you see how all the lines point in the same direction? That's because the gradients are all + 2. The bit that makes the difference is the constant at the end of the equation, which tells you where the lines cross over the y axis. For instance $y = 2x − 3$ cuts through the y axis at $y = −3$ because that's the y value when $x = 0$.

How to solve two equations at once with a graph

Phew! All these gradients and things are thirsty work, so let's abandon all sense of taste and catch up with Pongo at his Deluxe Burger bar. Pongo seems to be otherwise occupied for a moment, so let's check the board to see what tea and coffee cost...

Oh, dear. The prices have been obscured by a discarded kipper-and-pumpkin-flavour burger so we'll work it out. We'll let "y" be the price of a cup of tea and "x" be the price of a coffee. Now let's ask a couple of satisfied customers what they paid.

Aha! We can make these into two little equations. First we have $y + x = 70$. As we're going to plot it on a graph we need "$y =$" by itself on one side, so we adjust it to get $y = 70 - x$. This equation has two unknowns so we can't solve it by itself, but luckily the second

136

customer gave us $2y = x + 20$. If we divide both sides by 2 we get $y = \frac{x}{2} + 10$.

Now we've got *two* equations with two unknowns. These are called **simultaneous equations** and there are several different ways to solve them. You'll find other ways later in the "Double Trouble" chapter, but for now we're going to look at the fun way. All we need to do is draw the line for each equation on the same graph!

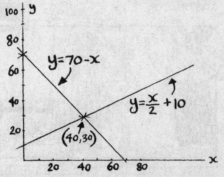

You'll see the lines cross over at (40,30) so $x = 40$ and $y = 30$. At this exact point the values for x and y work for both equations at once, and so amazingly enough this gives us the answer! Coffee costs 40p and tea costs 30p. We can check these prices with what the customers told us.

What IS going on?

Brace yourself for the ghastly truth. It seems that Pongo is keen to push back the frontiers of catering technology so he's round the back of his van inventing the "Loveburger". The idea is that this burger will taste so yummy, the terribly lovely Veronica Gumfloss only has to take one bite and she will melt into his arms. Pongo's ever-supportive mates are there to test his efforts.

Sadly for Pongo, he hasn't quite perfected that sublime blend of flavours yet, but you have to admire the way that rhubarb-and-sprout burger landed right in the dustbin. Amazingly enough, you can trace out the exact path of how the burger flew through the air using an equation! (The posh word for the burger's path is **trajectory**.)

When you throw something like one of Pongo's burgers, as it goes up and down, the force of earth's gravity makes it fly in a curve called a **parabola.** Sadly it isn't an *exact* parabola because of air resistance, but Pongo's burgers are so solid that the effect of the air is too tiny to make much of a difference. The very simplest equation that describes a parabola is this: $y = x^2$.

If you just have a plain "x" in your equation you always get straight lines on graphs, but as soon as you have a power such as x^2 you get a curve. These are fun to draw, so let's do a table for $y = x^2$ and then see what we get:

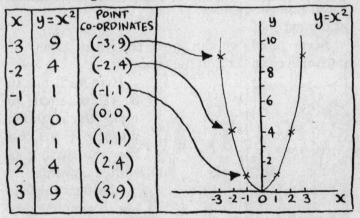

x	$y = x^2$	POINT CO-ORDINATES
-3	9	(-3, 9)
-2	4	(-2, 4)
-1	1	(-1, 1)
0	0	(0, 0)
1	1	(1, 1)
2	4	(2, 4)
3	9	(3, 9)

When you've got enough points to see what's going on, use all your arty skill to join them up with as neat a curve as you can. You'll see that $y = x^2$ gives us a nice "U" shape.

139

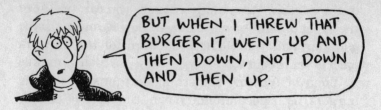

BUT WHEN I THREW THAT BURGER IT WENT UP AND THEN DOWN, NOT DOWN AND THEN UP.

True. Although the curve is the right shape, we need to move it around by slightly adjusting the equation. If we make it into $y = -x^2$, we'll get the same curve but it will be upside down.

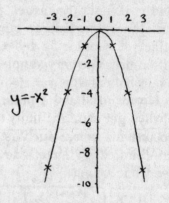

$y = -x^2$

However, it's a pity the x axis goes across at the top.

Never mind, we can move the x axis about by putting a constant into the equation.

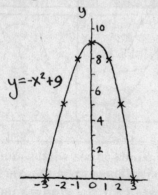

$y = -x^2 + 9$

Here we'll put in a +9 constant to make the equation into $y = -x^2 + 9$. See how the curve gets shifted upwards.

Aha! Now the lads are all sampling new variations on the Loveburger. We can see what happens to each burger with some special equations.

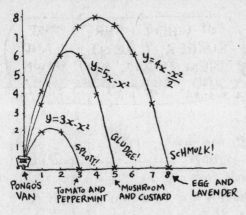

All these equations have got an x^2 term which makes sure we get the parabola shape.

Instead of a constant such as $+9$, we've put in an x term which makes all the curves go through the $(0,0)$ point – which is where Pongo has parked his van. So finally it's decision time:

While Pongo gets on with it, let's have a quick look at some more complicated equations on graphs. We've seen that x^2 gives one curve, but if you have $y = x^3$ you get a double curve like a nice reverse "S" shape…

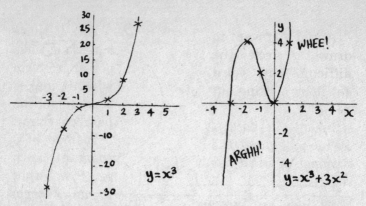

...and if you have $y = x^3 + 3x^2$ you've nearly got a roller coaster.

A really strange one is $y = \frac{1}{x}$ because you get *two* curves that don't touch the axes. You can't see what y is when $x = 0$. In fact, the answer is y is *plus OR minus infinity* at the same time! ARGHHH! This is when maths gets so murderous that it could damage the fabric of the Universe, so how do we avoid it happening?

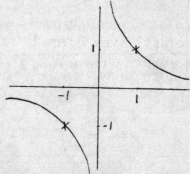

PSSST! LOOK! IT'S THE FIFTH AND FINAL RULE!

Rule 5: You must never divide by zero.

And if you want to draw a circle the difficult way, you'd get it by plotting out $x^2 + y^2 = 1$.

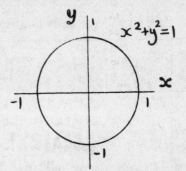

Meanwhile, back at Pongo's van, the moment of truth has arrived.

And so we've reached our last graph in this chapter:

You'll notice the Loveburger equation didn't have an x^2 term. This is because the intensity of Veronica's tantrum was enough to disrupt the Earth's gravity and allow the loveburger to fly straight up into deep space.

Parabolas

Here's a strange thought: what do car headlamps, secret listening devices, radio telescopes and flying burgers have in common? The answer is the parabola. We've already seen how gravity makes things fly in parabolic curves, but look at this:

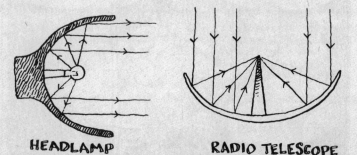

HEADLAMP   RADIO TELESCOPE

There's a very special position in the middle of a parabola called the "focus". If you were standing on the focus inside a giant parabola, you could throw a ball at any part of the parabola you like, and it would bounce straight out of the open end. This is why car headlamps and big spotlights use parabolic-shaped reflectors with a bulb at the focus. Every bit of light from the bulb hits the reflector and then shoots out in the same direction. That's how you get a nice tight beam of light.

A secret listening device works the opposite way because it has a parabolic dish with a microphone at the focus. If you aim it at somebody a long way off, the dish collects sound coming from that direction and bounces it into the focus. Therefore, the microphone picks up the sound you want and very little else.

A radio telescope works like the listening device. When it is pointed at any object up in space, the dish helps to collect as much information as possible while ignoring everything else. Let's see what this one's looking at.

146

DOUBLE TROUBLE

If you've got one equation with one unknown then you can usually solve it. If you've got one equation with two unknowns, then you're probably stuck. But if you have *two* equations with the same two unknowns, you're in with a chance. A pair of equations like this are called **simultaneous equations** and we met some on page 136. A quick ride on the Brownpool-on-Sea Scenic Railway will show what we mean.

So far this morning, the train has been to Fastbuck and back, and then gone to Grimethorpe where it stopped. In total, it's travelled 19 miles.

If we call the distance to Fastbuck "f" miles and the distance to Grimethorpe "g" miles we can make an equation: $2f + g = 19$

Unfortunately, this doesn't tell us enough to work out how far away Grimethorpe and Fastbuck are, so we'll check on what happened yesterday. The train went to Grimethorpe and back twice and then went to Fastbuck and finished there. In total it did 34 miles, so we get: $4g + f = 34$

We now have two equations with two unknowns. We have a choice of two different ways to solve them. Before we start, we'll write them out again and call them equation A and equation B.

$$A:\ 2f + g = 19$$
$$B:\ 4g + f = 34$$

Substitution

This is usually the easiest way to solve simultaneous equations. There are three jobs to do:

● Adjust one of the equations so that one of the letters is by itself on the left hand side. Here we'll take equation A and swap it round to get: $g = 19 - 2f$

● Substitute this letter in the other equation. So we'll take equation B and swap "g" for $(19 - 2f)$. We get: $4(19 - 2f) + f = 34$, which only has one unknown, so we can solve it!

    Open up the bracket: $4 \times 19 - 4 \times 2f + f = 34$

    Multiply the bits: $76 - 8f + f = 34$

    Get the f terms to one side: $-7f = 34 - 76$

    Multiply both sides by -1: $7f = 42$

    Divide through by 7: $f = 6$

● Now we know what f is, we can put this value into either equation and work out g. So if you look at equation A with $2f + g = 19$, you get $2 \times 6 + g = 19$, making $12 + g = 19$, so $g = 19 - 12 = 7$.

There's the answer! $f = 6$ and $g = 7$. You can test this by putting the numbers into equation B and seeing if they work.

Elimination

If you're feeling brave, you can also solve simultaneous equations by adding *whole* equations to each other to get rid of one of the letters. This takes skill, nerve and practice so first let's remind ourselves of what the equations are: A: $2f + g = 19$ and B: $4g + f = 34$

The clever bit is to adjust your equations so that when you add them a letter disappears. In this case we're going to get rid of letter "g", so we'll multiply everything in equation A by 4 and also multiply everything in equation B by –1. (Don't worry, it'll all make sense in a moment!)

A × 4: $8f + 4g = 76$

B × –1: $-4g - f = -34$

Notice that we've got + $4g$ in the top equation and – $4g$ in the bottom one! We can now add the two equations together. We add the two left-hand sides and the two right-hand sides.

We get: $8f + 4g - 4g - f = 76 - 34$

POW! $7f = 42$ so $f = 6$

Just like before, once we've solved one letter, we can plonk it into either equation – A or B – and work out the other one.

Once again, we find it's 7 miles to Grimethorpe and 6 miles to Fastbuck.

So there you have the two different ways to solve simultaneous equations.

THAT'S NOT QUITE TRUE. DON'T FORGET WE SAW ANOTHER WAY TO SOLVE SIMULTANEOUS EQUATIONS USING A GRAPH BACK ON PAGE 137.

The Fastbuck Gazette
TIDE REFUSES TO COME IN

Visitors to Fastbuck Bay have been alarmed to see the sea is keeping its distance.

Apparently, the River Puke has brought a tiny bit too much toxic sludge from our beloved factories down to the beach and now the tide is refusing to come in and wash it away.

"The sea is just being silly," declared Councillor M Bezzell yesterday. "I would like to reassure our citizens that it is perfectly safe to swim in black water containing three-eyed fish and talking seaweed."

Councillor M Bezzell :
"I went swimming and it didn't do me any harm."

The Foul City of Fastbuck is facing a serious crisis. If visitors are deterred from bringing their money into the town, then the councillors will have less to spend on important items such as big fancy cars and posh foreign holidays. Obviously something must be done, and so the council have decided to organize an emergency fact-finding mission.

There are only 100 councillors to do all the vital work required of them and they have split themselves into three teams.

- The first team of councillors will spend the afternoon going along the scenic railway to Brownpool-on-Sea and looking into the bay to check how much toxic sludge is being discharged.
- The second team of councillors will meet the factory owners at the Hightipps Hotel and have a fact-finding eight-course dinner followed by a cabaret act and dancing.
- The third team of councillors have to check that the toxic sludge isn't being spread across the world. Therefore, they will need to fly to Hawaii with their families and secretaries on a fleet of private jets and spend a month living in an exclusive beach resort to check that no toxic waste is washed ashore.

Obviously these trips cost money, and so the taxpayers of Fastbuck have demanded to know exactly how many councillors are to be on each team.

Ha! The councillors thought they could dazzle everyone with this jumble of numbers and letters, but with a bit of Murderous Maths detective work, we can discover what's really going on.

The first equation tells us that the total number of councillors, "C", is 100. When these councillors are split into the three teams, the number of people on the first team = c_1, the number on the second team = c_2 and the number on the third team = c_3. Notice that when we put a tiny number down at the bottom after a letter, it doesn't have anything to do with the actual sums. So, c_2 means the number of councillors in the second team, but c^2 would mean $c \times c$.

So what we've got is *three* equations with three unknowns, and we should be able to solve them and find out what c_1, c_2 and c_3 are before the councillors return. We'll call our equations A, B and C.

$$\text{A: } c_1 + c_2 + c_3 = 100$$
$$\text{B: } c_1 = 19c_2 - c_3$$
$$\text{C: } c_3 = 21c_2 - 11c_1$$

Let's rearrange A to get $c_1 = 100 - c_2 - c_3$

We can now put this value of c_1 into equation B:
$100 - c_2 - c_3 = 19c_2 - c_3$

We've got lucky! There's $- c_3$ on both sides so we can just cancel them both out. We're left with $100 - c_2 = 19c_2$, which quickly becomes $20c_2 = 100$. If we divide both sides by 20, we get $c_2 = 5$. That means five councillors are having the fact-finding dinner.

Meanwhile, our investigations continue.

If we swap c_2 with 5 in equation A we get:

$$c_1 + 5 + c_3 = 100$$

We'll tidy this up and call it equation D:

$$c_1 + c_3 = 95$$

And if we swap c_2 with 5 in equation C we get:

$$c_3 = 21 \times 5 - 11c_1$$

Which we'll make into equation E:

$$c_3 = 105 - 11c_1$$

Now we've got two equations with two unknowns and it's easy. If you look at equation D, you can subtract c_1 from both sides and make it into: $c_3 = 95 - c_1$

You then substitute this into equation E to get:

$$95 - c_1 = 105 - 11c_1$$

Shuffle it around:

$$11c_1 - c_1 = 105 - 95$$
$$10c_1 = 10$$

And finally:

$$c_1 = 1$$

So we can now report that the "team" that went along the scenic railway had only one councillor – Mr Pinkerton.

So how many councillors went to Hawaii? Of our 100 councillors, five had dinner and one trainspotted, so 94 are in Hawaii. You can double-check by swapping c_1 with 1 in equation E and you'll get $c_3 = 105 - 11 \times 1$ so $c_3 = 105 - 11 = 94$.

Luckily, this is only a Murderous Maths book and nothing like this ever happens in real life, which is just as well because the only councillor who came up with any sort of useful solution to the polluted beach crisis was Mr Pinkerton.

The Fastbuck Gazette
TOURISTS FLOCK TO SEE COUNCIL CLEAN UP

Thousands of thrilled tourists returned today to Fastbuck to see the old council members licking the beach clean after they had been caught taking free holidays at the taxpayers' expense.

The new President Pinkerton was asked if he enjoyed watching his disgraced ex-comrades' shame. "I'm lapping it up," he joked. "And it's all thanks to some Murderous Maths."

THE ZERO PROOF

You've come through some of the roughest and toughest maths invented so at last it's time to see if you're ready to do serious battle against the unknown. There's a very nasty little piece of algebra called "The Zero Proof", which is usually kept guarded in an isolation bunker somewhere underneath one of the Murderous Maths Organization's executive golf courses. The ZP looks innocent enough, but if it got out of control it could threaten the entire universe and everything in it.

*Your challenge is to work out how to disarm the ZP.
I was going to have you fetched in a special limousine
with blacked-out windows so that you couldn't see
where you were going, but unfortunately the location
is SO secret that even the driver isn't allowed to see
where he's going. As a result, he crashed the car into
the water hazard on the 14th hole.*

*So, I'm going to take a big risk. I'm going to put the
ZP into this book but please bear in mind that it's SO
SECRET you should look at it with your eyes shut. At
first glance it looks like this:*

But if you open your eyes a tiny bit it looks like this:

The ZERO Proof

- We pick any two numbers that are the same. We'll call them a and b.
- If a and b are the same, we can write: $a = b$
  Remember, we can do what we like as long as we treat both sides of the equation in exactly the same way.
- Multiply both sides by a: $\qquad\qquad a^2 = ab$
- Subtract b^2 from both sides: $\qquad a^2 - b^2 = ab - b^2$
- On the left-hand side we've got $a^2 - b^2$ which is the difference of two squares. We found out back on page 108 that we can write this as $(a - b)(a + b)$. Then on the right-hand side we can factorize the $ab - b^2$ into $b(a - b)$.
  Our equation becomes: $\qquad (a - b)(a + b) = b(a - b)$
- Divide both sides by $(a - b)$: $\qquad (a + b) = b$
- Get rid of the bracket: $\qquad\qquad a + b = b$
- Subtract b from both sides: $\qquad a + b - b = b - b$
- And therefore: $\qquad\qquad\qquad\quad a = 0$
  We didn't say what number "a" was to start with, so "a" could be anything. Therefore, we've proved that any number equals zero.

This is EXTREMELY dangerous stuff! If you can prove that any number = 0 then everything collapses. Think about it: 10 tonnes of solid rock become nothing, 100 years of time disappear in an instant, a distance of a million light years shrinks to zero. We live in one world, but if you prove that 1 = 0 then the world disappears!

If you don't believe the power of the ZP then look at the bottom of the last page. Even the numbers on the page that contain this catastrophic calculation have already turned to 0.

However, if you've been following this book carefully, you'll realize why the ZP is not allowed to wreak its havoc on an unsuspecting planet. I'll give you a couple of clues … remember the proof started with $a = b$ so what does $(a - b)$ equal? If that doesn't give you the answer then look back through the pages and check rule five! (When you find it, blow a final triumphant fanfare and then do a big finish by slapping your head with the book: BASH!)

As for me, the Phantom X, it's time to slip back into the shadows and continue the battle against the unknown. But this time, it's different. Thanks to you, I know that I'm no longer working alone. So, farewell, it's been fun. Goodbye for ever … and good luck!